MUSIC IN CATHOLIC LITURGY

A Pastoral and Theological Companion to *Sing to the Lord*

Gerald Dennis Gill

HillenbrandBooks

Chicago / Mundelein, Illinois

MUSIC IN CATHOLIC LITURGY: A PASTORAL AND THEOLOGICAL COMPANION TO SING TO THE LORD © 2009 Archdiocese of Chicago: Liturgy Training Publications, 3949 South Racine Avenue, Chicago IL 60609; 1-800-933-1800, fax 1-800-933-7094, e-mail orders@ltp.org. All rights reserved. See our Web site at www.LTP.org.

Hillenbrand Books is an imprint of Liturgy Training Publications (LTP) and the Liturgical Institute at the University of Saint Mary of the Lake (USML). The imprint is focused on contemporary and classical theological thought concerning the liturgy of the Catholic Church. Available at bookstores everywhere, through LTP by calling 1-800-933-1800, or visiting www.LTP.org. Further information about the **Hillenbrand Books** publishing program is available from the University of Saint Mary of the Lake/ Mundelein Seminary, 1000 East Maple Avenue, Mundelein, IL 60060 (847-837-4542), on the Web at www.usml.edu/liturgicalinstitute, or e-mail litinst@usml.edu.

Cover photo © The Crosiers/Gene Plaisted, osc

Printed in the United Stated of America.

Library of Congress Control Number: 2009927751

13 12 11 10   6 5 4 3 2

978-1-59525-028-5

HMCL

Contents

Preface

The Fathers of the Second Vatican Council (1962–1965) continue
to teach us with the enduring words of the *Constitution on the Sacred
Liturgy* (*Sacrosanctum concilium*). This is some of what the Fathers
taught about liturgical music:

> The musical tradition of the universal Church is a treasure of inestimable
> value, greater even than that of any other art. The main reason for this
> preeminence is that, as sacred song united to the words, it forms a neces-
> sary or integral part of the solemn liturgy. . . . [S]acred music will be
> more holy the more closely it is joined to the liturgical rite, whether by
> adding delight to prayer, fostering oneness of spirit or investing the rites
> with greater solemnity. . . . [L]iturgical service takes on a more noble
> aspect when the rites are celebrated with singing. . . (SC 112 and 113).

These phrases from chapter 6 of the *Constitution on the Sacred
Liturgy* set in clear relief the fundamental significance and role
of liturgical music in Roman Catholic worship. Liturgical music
is the vestment for the liturgical text—song united to the words.
As such, liturgical music, that is, music which is truly at the service
of the text—closely connected with the liturgical action—renders
the celebrations of the Mysteries of the Lord more fitting, more noble.
Liturgical music externally expresses with a singular capacity the faith
revealed in the words and rites of the Sacred Liturgy.

The Church in our country from the time of the Council
has made great strides as it continues to refine the application of these
insights on liturgical music. The United States Bishops' document
Sing to the Lord: Music in Divine Worship represents a new stage in this
ongoing refinement with an even greater awareness of the significance
and role of liturgical music in Roman Catholic worship. *Sing to the
Lord* guides pastors and liturgical music ministers anew to bring about
more fully what the Council Fathers taught about liturgical music,
especially as "a necessary or integral part of the solemn liturgy."

The editors at Hillenbrand Books contacted me soon after *Sing
to the Lord* was approved by our American Bishops to provide a type
of guide for this new music document. I enthusiastically accepted the

opportunity to write this companion with the hope that it would provide for a wide readership—priests, deacons, seminarians, music ministers and musicians, and interested people from other ecclesial communions—a way to read *Sing to the Lord* with a more complete theological and liturgical perspective. This book expands on *Sing to the Lord* with additional reflections on the nature and purpose of liturgical music as well as a more thorough presentation of the use of liturgical music in all of the liturgical rites.

I have been greatly assisted in writing this book by Sister Marganne Drago, a Sister of Saint Joseph of Philadelphia. Sister Marganne brought the unique experience of many years as a professional music educator and parish music minister to the pages of this book, as well as a persisting spirit to complete the project. I am most grateful for her contributions, her careful review of the work, and her abiding commitment to the promotion of authentic liturgical music.

Kevin Thornton of Hillenbrand Books proved to be a most patient and understanding editor throughout the progress of this book. I am grateful to Kevin for his excitement about this project from start to finish, for his own professional review of the work, and most of all for quickly seeing a way to promote *Sing to the Lord* effectively.

Father Joshua R. Brommer, a priest of the Diocese of Harrisburg, with the eyes of both a parish priest and liturgical musician, offered many helpful suggestions so that this book could better serve its purpose as a theological and liturgical companion to *Sing to the Lord*. Sister Margaret Louise Garvin, also a Sister of Saint Joseph of Philadelphia, provided a careful grammar and punctuation check of the initial draft of this book. Ms. Constance Scharff, staff of the office for the formation of the laity of the Archdiocese of Philadelphia, also provided a careful grammar and punctuation check of a later draft of the book. I would also like to thank Linda Cerebona, a twenty-five-year veteran of parish ministry and the Music Director at University of St. Mary of the Lake, and Father John Szmyd, the Director of Liturgy at the University of St. Mary of the Lake, for their careful reading of the manuscript and their useful suggestions. Robert Demke provided a careful and thoughtful reading of the final draft.

I have a vivid memory of one of my mentors in my study of the Sacred Liturgy describing with awe his participation in a liturgical procession. He profoundly sensed as he walked with others in this procession that he was also walking with Christ in history, walking with him presently and walking with him in glory. I listened intently to my professor's experience with a question in my mind: How does this happen? He answered my unspoken query as he continued, it was the music, the music we sang as we processed. I hope as you read this book you will see and understand, in a convincing way, just how liturgical music, as much as "it adds delight to prayer, fosters unity of minds or confers greater solemnity upon the sacred rites," opens to us more fully the mysteries we celebrate for the worship of God and for our share in his divine life.

Introduction

THE BISHOPS' NEW DOCUMENT

Sing to the Lord: Music in Divine Worship, as the title of this new
document by the Bishops of the United States, gives a clear directive
for understanding the role and significance of liturgical music.
Liturgical music, as with all that makes up the celebration of the
Sacred Liturgy, is for the worship of Almighty God. *Sing to the Lord:
Music in Divine Worship* deserves to be read, understood, and applied
with this renewed approach by all who sing the Sacred Liturgy, by
all the clergy and all the faithful, and especially those engaged in the
ministry of liturgical music.

A quick glance at the Table of Contents of *Sing to the Lord*[1]
shows us five main parts which indicate a carefully crafted outline of
its theological and liturgical development. Part I, "Why We Sing,"
describes the nature of song, song as a gift from God and for the glory
of God in worship, especially Christian worship, which impels those
who worship the Triune God to sing his praises and to recognize
singing as a fundamental way to participate in divine worship. Part II,
"The Church at Prayer," underscores the constitution of the Church
with a description of those in Holy Orders and the baptized, with
special attention given to ministers of liturgical music, with guidance
to carry out their roles to promote a sung celebration of the Sacred
Liturgy with competence. Part II also considers those in specific
leadership and formation roles in liturgical music, as well as music
in Catholic Schools, diverse cultures and languages, and the use
of the Latin language in the Sacred Liturgy. Part III, "The Music
of Catholic Worship," presents the broad topic of music in Catholic
worship, both in terms of the different kinds of music for the
Sacred Liturgy and the many instruments that can be used for musical
support. Additionally, Part III offers some information on the location of musicians and their instruments, acoustics, copyrights, and
participation aids. Part IV, "Preparing Music for Catholic Worship,"

---

1. Throughout this book, the abbreviated title *Sing to the Lord* also will be used instead of the
complete title, *Sing to the Lord: Music in Divine Worship*.

focuses on the parts sung during the celebration of the Sacred Liturgy, those who prepare the music, the careful choice of music and judging the qualities of music for the Sacred Liturgy. Part Five, "The Musical Structure of Catholic Worship," builds on the theological and liturgical foundations established in the preceding chapters. It identifies the music in the celebration of the Mass, the other Sacraments, the Liturgy of the Hours, and other liturgical rites and devotions.

The sources for *Sing to the Lord* include the majority of the English language ritual books, the *Lectionary for Mass*, the general instructions for the *Roman Missal* and the *Liturgy of the Hours*, and several documents of the Second Vatican Council. The *Catechism of the Catholic Church* is occasionally referenced in the Bishops' text. More to the point, *Sing to the Lord* includes the expected magisterial documents on sacred music from the period immediately prior to the Second Vatican Council (1962–1965) up to and including Pope Benedict XVI's synodal exhortation *Sacramentum caritatis* (2007). The United States Bishops' statements *Music in Catholic Worship* (1972) and *Liturgical Music Today* (1982) as well as the Bishops' statements *Built of Living Stones: Art, Architecture and Worship* (2000) and *Co-Workers in the Vineyard of the Lord: A Resource for Guiding the Development of Lay Ecclesial Ministry* (2005) are also referenced.

DEVELOPMENT AND FORCE OF *SING TO THE LORD: MUSIC IN DIVINE WORSHIP*

The Bishops' publication of *Sing to the Lord* responds to the pressing need to provide current guidelines for singing the Sacred Liturgy, especially with a renewed fervor for authentic celebrations. Perhaps the word "authentic" needs some explanation. In more recent times, especially with increased theological reflection on the celebration of the Sacred Liturgy, there is a recovered understanding that the norms that govern its celebration ensure a genuine participation in the Mystery actually celebrated. "The primary way to foster the participation of the People of God in the sacred rite is the proper celebration of the rite itself."[2] Thus, authentic celebrations are those which faithfully adhere to the norms, directives, and intent of the liturgical books and documents.

Part of the pressing need for *Sing to the Lord* stems from the promulgation of the third edition of the *Missale Romanum* and its general instruction in 2002 along with universal documents such as the *Chirograph for the Centenary of the motu proprio Tra le sollecitudini* of Pope John Paul II (2003) and *Sacramentum caritatis*.

In June 2001, a Subcommittee on Music and the Liturgy of the Committee on the Liturgy was revived as authorized by the United States Conference of Catholic Bishops. This subcommittee first developed a *Directory on Music and the Liturgy* which was approved in 2006 in accord with number 108 of *Liturgiam Authenticam* (2001). This same subcommittee then undertook the task of revising the 1972 *Music in Catholic Worship*, receiving a wide cross-section of input from various liturgists and musicians around the United States. It was the original intention of the Committee on the Liturgy to ask the Bishops of the United States to approve the revision of *Music in Catholic Worship* in the form of particular law. In the end, this revision, as developed by the Committee on Divine Worship (formerly, the Committee on the Liturgy) of the United States Conference of Catholic Bishops, was approved by the full body of Bishops of the United States as their own statement or document and not as particular law on November 14, 2007, for publication with the title *Sing to the Lord: Music in Divine Worship*.

Sing to the Lord: Music in Divine Worship therefore replaces its thirty-five year old antecedent, *Music in Catholic Worship*. These new guidelines on music and the Liturgy, as stated by the Bishops in the first few sentences of the new document, "are designed to provide direction to those preparing for the celebration of the sacred Liturgy according to the current liturgical books (in the ordinary form of celebration)."[3]

These new guidelines, however, have a twofold context. The first context is explicitly mentioned in the Foreword of the new document. As this Foreword begins with greetings from the Bishops

2. SCar 38.
3. STL, p. x.

to those collaborators in Holy Orders, those with ministries in liturgical music and all the faithful, there is also the reminder from these same Bishops of "[their] duty and [their] joy as shepherds of the Church to guide and oversee liturgical song in each particular Church."[4] As it is consistently stated elsewhere, for example in the *General Instruction of the Roman Missal*[5], it belongs to the diocesan Bishop, who is the chief steward of the mysteries of God in the particular Church, the moderator, promoter, and guardian of the whole of its liturgical life, to safeguard, direct, and ensure the singing of the sacred Liturgy as its dignity and nature requires.

The second context is perhaps implied but needs to be stated here more explicitly. These new guidelines, as an aid to the duty and joy of the Bishops, further the application of the norms and principles established for liturgical music as found in the liturgical books, their introductions, and specific liturgical documents. Concretely this application of the norms and principles for liturgical music requires a shared commitment to them on the part of the local Bishop with his priests, deacons, and liturgical music ministers. The responsibilities of each—Bishop, priests, deacons, and liturgical music ministers—are discussed more fully in Chapter 2 of this book. For now, it is sufficient to note the duty of all to know, honor, and apply the Church's directives for liturgical music. Therefore, the binding force of *Sing to the Lord: Music in Divine Worship* is established with the publication under the pastoral leadership of the Bishops for the promotion of authentic celebrations of the Sacred Liturgy. Also, this same force continues with its repetition of what is already found in various other sources of liturgical norms and law, specifically in the liturgical books. Finally, the reception and implementation of this new document will assist the Church in the United States to sing the earthly Liturgy with a faith, reverence, and authenticity inspired

---

4. STL, Foreword.

5. See GIRM 22, in part, "The Bishop should therefore be determined that the priests, the deacons, and the lay Christian faithful grasp ever more deeply the genuine meaning of the rites and liturgical texts, and thereby be led to an active and fruitful celebration of the Eucharist. To the same end, he should also be vigilant that the dignity of these celebrations be enhanced. In promoting this dignity, the beauty of the sacred place, of music, and of art should contribute as greatly as possible." See CD 15; see also SC 41.

by the heavenly Liturgy, to sing today the song that sounds forever among the angels and saints.

PASTORAL RATIONALE FOR THIS THEOLOGICAL AND LITURGICAL COMPANION

Sing to the Lord belongs to a new series of statements and reflections on aspects of liturgical celebrations. This new document has the benefit of more than a generation of use of the reformed rites consequent to the Second Vatican Council, the promulgation of a new edition of the *Roman Missal* with its revised general instruction, magisterial directives on the celebration of the Sacred Liturgy, maturing theological reflection on liturgical music, and a process for its composition, including widespread interest and competent contributors. *Sing to the Lord*, as the revision statement of *Music in Catholic Worship*, improves on its predecessor in many remarkable ways and promises to better guide the most important task of providing authentic liturgical music in the Church in the United States.

Precisely because *Sing to the Lord* arrives at a time of continuing development and reflection in the course of the ongoing renewal of the celebration of the Sacred Liturgy and is the project of input from a variety of persons during this period, its language at times results in an uneven tone as it attempts to bridge some real differences in ideas. For some of us it may be a whole new type of document and be difficult at times to read and follow. It is hoped that this companion will be useful in appreciating the depth and breadth of the U.S. Bishops' statement. For all of us in the Church in the United States, *Sing to the Lord* begins a new period for a more profound understanding of why and what we sing in the Sacred Liturgy.

This book in your hands is a theological and liturgical companion to *Sing to the Lord: Music in Divine Worship*. Reading and applying this companion, especially on the part of pastors and those engaged in liturgical music ministries, will promote the effectiveness of the twofold context for *Sing to the Lord* as mentioned above, namely, the Bishops' duty to direct the singing of the Sacred Liturgy and the faithful application of norms for liturgical music.

For this reason, this companion, with an emphasis on a theological and liturgical reading of *Sing to the Lord*, closely follows the contents of the new document. As stated earlier, the given outline of *Sing to the Lord* indicates a theological ordering to its presentation which this companion further illustrates. This book offers you, the reader, a more complete presentation and explanation of the liturgical points identified and highlighted by *Sing to the Lord*.

A more detailed overview of the organization of this book may be helpful at this point. This book consists of three principal parts: Part I, Music and the Liturgy: Its Purpose, Its Singers, and Its Expression; Part II, Liturgical Music: Its Patterns and Choices; and Part III, Singing the Eucharist, the Other Sacraments, and Other Liturgical Rites.

Part I includes three chapters. Chapter 1, "The Purpose of Liturgical Music," looks at topics such as liturgical music, the purpose of singing the liturgy and liturgical participation. Chapter 2, "The Singers of Liturgical Music," presents the formation requirements of those who sing the Sacred Liturgy, that is, the clergy and the baptized, especially liturgical music ministers. Leadership and formation in music ministry, including Catholic Education, cultural and language considerations, as well as the use of Latin are also considered. Chapter 3, "The Ways to Express Liturgical Music," describes the quality of liturgical music, Gregorian chant, vernacular liturgical music and instruments.

Part II includes two chapters. Chapter 4, "What is Progressive Solemnity?" outlines this principle with its application. Chapter 5, "What to Sing During the Sacred Liturgy?" includes topics such as the parts to be sung and planning those parts and the qualities of liturgical music.

Part III includes four chapters. Chapter 6, "How do we Sing the Eucharist?"; Chapter 7, "How do we Sing the Other Sacraments?"; Chapter 8, "How do we Sing the Liturgy of the Hours?"; Chapter 9, "How do we Sing Other Liturgical Rites?," all follow the same pattern. Each chapter gives a detailed overview according to the respective liturgical books and with constant reference to *Sing to the Lord* for singing the actual liturgical celebrations.

In addition to the sources already referenced in *Sing to the Lord*, this book additionally relies on the *Roman Missal* (the *Sacramentary*), the introduction to the *Lectionary for Mass*, the *Liturgy of the Hours*, the *Ordo Cantus Missae*, and the Church's given song books (notably the *Graduale Romanum* and the *Graduale Simplex*).

    This book provides a more thorough theological and liturgical reading of *Sing to the Lord* and promises to be a useful tool for all those involved in the preparation of the sung celebration of the Sacred Liturgy. The readers of this book are the parish priests, deacons, seminarians, and members of the faithful. Of course, those of you who are liturgical music ministers are a special audience for this book. This timely, new and comprehensive response to *Sing to the Lord: Music in Divine Worship* is one more help to sing the faith we celebrate.

Abbreviations

CCC   *Catechism of the Catholic Church*

DPPL   *Directory on Popular Piety and the Liturgy: Principles and Guidelines*

GILOH   *General Instruction of the Liturgy of the Hours*

GIRM   *General Instruction of the Roman Missal*

HCWEM   *Holy Communion and Worship of the Eucharist Outside Mass*

LFM   *Lectionary for Mass*

MS   *Musicam sacram*

MSD   *Musicae Sacrae Disciplina*

OCM   *Order of Celebrating Marriage*

OCF   *Order of Christian Funerals*

PCS   *Pastoral Care of the Sick*

PS   *Paschale Solemnitatis: On Preparing and Celebrating the Easter Feasts*

RBC   *Rite of Baptism for Children*

RC   *Rite of Confirmation*

RO   *Rites of Ordination*

RP   *Rite of Penance*

RCIA	*Rite of Christian Initiation of Adults*
RM	*Roman Missal*
SC	*Constitution on the Sacred Liturgy (Sacrosanctum concilium)*
SCar	*Sacramentum caritatis*
SCAP	*Sunday Celebrations in the Absence of a Priest*
STL	*Sing to the Lord*
TLS	*Tra le sollecitudini*

Part I

Music and the Liturgy: Its Purpose, Its Singers, and Its Expression

Sing to the Lord: Music in Divine Worship in its first three parts provides an important theological overview. The topics of these three parts include:
- singing, especially singing the Sacred Liturgy;
- the formation and duties of the members of the Church when singing the liturgy; and
- music in Roman Catholic worship.

The discussion of these points provides the necessary foundation and background for the more practical discussions that follow on the preparation to sing the Liturgy. In Part I of this book, we develop these same three topics from *Sing to the Lord* to enhance their theological focus for you, so that you may appreciate the theological reasons for liturgical practice, and especially liturgical music.

We encourage you to read the previous statements of the United States Bishops on music and the Liturgy, *Music in Catholic Worship* and *Liturgical Music Today* as part of the developmental background for *Sing to the Lord.* You will notice as you read these statements that there is a shift on many levels and with several ideas between the former documents and this new document. An important dimension to this shift is the newly presented theological underpinnings to liturgical music as described in *Sing to the*

Lord. These theological foundations make *Sing to the Lord* not just a new document but also a new look at liturgical music in the United States.[1]

---

1. Jan Michael Joncas offers a fine survey of what many of the previous documents on liturgical music, both universal and national documents, dating from Pius X's 1903 *Tra le sollecitudini* to the present, say about many of the topics raised in the first three sections of *Sing to the Lord* and explicated in this book. See Jan Michael Joncas. *From Sacred Song to Ritual Music: Twentieth-century Understanding of Roman Catholic Worship Music.* Collegeville: The Liturgical Press, 1997.

Chapter 1

The Purpose of Liturgical Music

INTRODUCTION

This Chapter considers two important questions:
- What is the theological purpose of singing the Liturgy? and,
- How does this singing assist our liturgical participation?

Before we are able to answer these two questions, we need to provide a brief description of the Sacred Liturgy and liturgical music.

WHAT IS THE SACRED LITURGY?

Today, it is quite possible to have as many answers to the question "what is the Liturgy?" as people asked to respond. And in most instances, their answers might only be a partial response. The *Catechism of the Catholic Church* provides a very helpful summary response to the question, what is the Sacred Liturgy:

> In the liturgy of the Church, it is principally his own Paschal mystery that Christ signifies and makes present. During his earthly life Jesus announced his Paschal mystery by his teaching and anticipated it by his actions. When his Hour comes, he lives out the unique event of history which does not pass away: Jesus dies, is buried, rises from the dead, and is seated at the right hand of the Father "once for all." His Paschal mystery is a real event that occurred in our history, but it is unique: all other historical events happen once, and then they pass away, swallowed up in the past. The Paschal mystery of Christ, by contrast, cannot remain only in the past, because by his death he destroyed death, and all that Christ is—all that he did and suffered for all men—participates in the divine eternity, and so transcends all times while being made present in them all.

The event of the Cross and Resurrection *abides* and draws everything toward life.[2] (CCC 1085)

The Sacred Liturgy is this event, a divine event, the event of the death and Resurrection of Jesus. The Liturgy both celebrates and is the Paschal Mystery of the Lord! Whenever the members of the Church are assembled to celebrate the Sacred Liturgy they participate in this unique divine event to give glory to God and in so doing receive a share in God's life and holiness.[3]

Such a clear and authentic understanding of the divine event which the Sacred Liturgy celebrates underscores the importance and dignity of all else that is said about the liturgical celebration in its various dimensions, most especially, liturgical music. This true understanding helps us to recognize that liturgical music also participates in divine worship!

WHAT IS LITURGICAL MUSIC?

Commonly, the music sung in the course of the celebration of the Sacred Liturgy receives several different labels. At times it is referred to as liturgical music or sacred music or even religious music. All three of these identifying tags carry a different meaning and describe distinct types of music even when on occasion sung during the Sacred Liturgy. Precise definitions are often lacking and at times the terms have been used interchangeably with varying meanings in documents and statements on music and the Liturgy over the last 50 years. A more precise description and presentation of sacred or religious music requires another discussion in light of what can be described as liturgical music. However, properly and specifically, the music prescribed for liturgical celebrations is called liturgical music.[4]

---

2. The CCC in its Part Two, Section One, provides a concise presentation of the Sacred Liturgy in its many dimensions. The CCC both synthesizes and develops the teaching in the *Constitution on the Sacred Liturgy* on the topic of the Sacred Liturgy. See CCC, 1066–1209.

3. See also SC 7.

4. Anthony Ruff provides a complete description of liturgical music in Part I of his work, *Sacred Music and Liturgical Reform*. See Anthony Ruff. *Sacred Music and Liturgical Reform: Treasures and Transformations*. Chicago: Hillenbrand Books, 2007.

Sing to the Lord makes use of the proper term liturgical music as do we throughout this book. *Sing to the Lord* does not describe its use of the term liturgical music, but in its use provides for its description. First and foremost, the presumption that the reformed rites of the Roman Rite are intrinsically musical, that is, are to be sung, begins the description of liturgical music. Liturgical music must include the given texts of the Liturgy. Secondly, the given texts of the liturgical rites are to be sung with the given tones. Thirdly, the psalter, above all the books of Sacred Scripture, and the liturgical books provide the principal content for liturgical musical texts. In summary, liturgical music is the singing of the liturgical texts themselves according to the given tones. The texts are those both in and indicated by the liturgical books. This accepted definition of liturgical music, the same implied by *Sing to the Lord,* is the one used in this book.

WHAT ARE SOME THEOLOGICAL PURPOSES FOR SINGING THE LITURGY?

In Part I, *Sing to the Lord* begins with a brief theological survey in response to the question "Why We Sing." The Bishops describe song as a gift, a gift from God. Since God dwells in each person and music has its source in each person, then God, who gives us song, is somehow present in the song (see STL 1).

And if this is the case, then music or song that arises from within the person, with song's origin in the Giver, leads the singer beyond the person to God. The song that comes forth from the person is at once personal and in its hearing also belongs to others. Thus, *Sing to the Lord* concludes that when this song occurs within the Church in the gathering of the liturgical assembly, with the song's origin in God, such singing becomes a sacramental presence of God to his people (see STL 2).

The Sacred Scriptures are replete with descriptions of God's people singing at times, even at the urging of God himself. Jesus sings with the Apostles and the Apostles themselves witness to the place of singing before the Lord (see STL 3, 4).[5]

---

5. STL provides excellent examples in the notes for numbers 3 and 4 of song in praise of God in the Sacred Scriptures.

Sing to the Lord makes the point that there is a relationship between God and song as well as the further point that singing among the Christian people disposes them to the divine presence as the scriptures testify. Thus, in *Sing to the Lord*, the answer to the question of Why we sing summarizes the theological purpose of singing the Liturgy as both strengthening faith and as a sacramental encounter.

The following passage from *Sing to the Lord* illustrates the first theological purpose of singing the Sacred Liturgy, strengthening faith:

> Obedient to Christ and to the Church, we gather in liturgical assembly, week after week. As our predecessors did, we find ourselves "singing psalms, hymns and spiritual songs with gratitude in [our] hearts to God."[6] This common sung expression of faith within liturgical celebrations strengthens our faith when it grows weak and draws us into the divinely inspired voice of the Church at prayer. Faith grows when it is well expressed in celebration. Good celebrations can foster and nourish faith. Poor celebrations may weaken it. Good music "make[s] the liturgical prayers of the Christian community more alive and fervent so that everyone can praise and beseech the Triune God more powerfully, more intently and more effectively.[7] (STL 5)

Christians from the very beginning assembled to worship God with the word of the Lord flowing from their hearts and sounding on their lips. In this common sung praise of God, Christians found strength as the song announced a common faith, with every weakness drawn into the strength of a oneness of the song and the faith. The music of the Liturgy must serve this commonality of song and faith; it must nourish and enrich both. In this way liturgical music will be oriented to Almighty God, that is, it will be the music of divine worship.

Another passage from *Sing to the Lord* illustrates the a second theological purpose of singing the Sacred Liturgy, a sacramental encounter:

---

6. Col 3:16; see *General Instruction of the Roman Missal* (GIRM), no. 39 (Washington, DC: United States Conference of Catholic Bishops [USCCB], 2003). See Eph 5:19. [Footnote in STL]

7. Musical Sacrae Disciplina (MSD), no. 31; see no. 33. [Footnote in STL]

"In human life, signs and symbols occupy an important place. As a being at once body and spirit, man expresses and perceives spiritual realities through physical signs and symbols. . . . Inasmuch as they are creatures, these perceptible realities can become means of expressing the action of God who sanctifies men, and the action of men who offer worship to God."[8] This sacramental principle is the consistent belief of the Church throughout history. In Liturgy, we use words, gestures, signs, and symbols to proclaim Christ's presence and to reply with our worship and praise. (STL 6)

All of life includes signs, indications, and pointers to other things. Sometimes these signs indicate the same or even greater realities. In a similar and borrowed way, Christians have likewise always benefited from the use of signs to indicate other realities, often times spiritual realities. We think of the Sacraments. These signs carry the real possibilities of manifesting the actions of God himself as well as our actions before God, especially the worship of Almighty God. Liturgical music is a sign like many of the other signs employed in the celebration of the Sacred Liturgy, an indication of God's action and our actions before God in divine worship.

Singing the Liturgy then makes a real difference! Singing the Sacred Liturgy, as has been and continues to be the liturgical tradition and practice of the Roman Rite, strengthens the faith of those who sing, the faith in the Mysteries celebrated and the faith that supports the active living of the Christian life. Singing is an encounter with the Lord! Singing is sacramental! Liturgical singing is one of the signs through which the spiritual realities celebrated in the Sacred Liturgy are both expressed and received by those who sing and listen.

Finally, especially in the rites of the Church's prayer, we sing our worship of God to join now and anticipate our privileged place from the seat of Baptism at the table of the Holy Eucharist in the eternal choir of those who have on their lips the primordial song of the Liturgy which is the Lord's canticle of victory over sin and death (see STL 7). Every time the Christian liturgical assembly sings the Sacred Liturgy, the new song of Christ sounds in heaven and earth. This is why we sing!

---

8. *Catechism of the Catholic Church* (CCC), 2nd ed., nos 1146, 1148 (Washington, DC: Libreria Editrice Vaticana–USCCB, 2000). [Footnote in STL]

We sing our faith to be strengthened in faith and encounter the One in whom we believe. This paschal song of the Liturgy does not end with its celebration; it is also the song of the Christian life (see STL 8).

Therefore, singing with such a purpose, the purpose of worship, the purpose of communion in Christ and his Paschal victory, encourages the Christian to bring this song into the everyday living of the Christian life. This is a life that begins and ends with Christ's song and attends to the announcement of the word of the Lord in the works of peace, justice, and charity. As the Bishops' document declares, "Particularly inspired by sung participation, the body of the Word Incarnate goes forth to spread the Gospel with full force and compassion." (STL 9)

What Is Liturgical Participation?

Sing to the Lord provides us with an authentic perspective on participation in the Sacred Liturgy—highlighting internal or, as some say, interior participation. In any discussion of liturgical participation, we recall the renewed impetus given by the *Constitution on the Sacred Liturgy*. The full and active participation of all in the Sacred Liturgy is the primary and indispensable source from which the faithful derive the true Christian spirit (see SC 14).[9] The *Constitution* repeats here what was earlier stated by Pope St. Pius X in his 1903 *motu proprio, Tra le sollecitudini*, and remained a consistent emphasis of the Liturgical Movement in the years leading up to the Second Vatican Council. (See TLS, Introduction) Liturgical participation fuels the living of the Christian life. This emphasis is especially important for pastors and liturgical music ministers who prepare the celebration of the Church's liturgical rites, especially the Sunday Eucharist. These celebrations assist the people to be open and disposed to the grace and gifts of the Mysteries of the Lord to respond to the Gospel in everyday life in an authentic way (see STL 10).

The Sacred Liturgy is a divine event. In the celebration of the Sacred Liturgy, God continues to speak his Word and manifest himself in the Sacraments to his people through the Church. All of

---

9. See also STL 11

this occurs with the ordained and the baptized, as the members
of the Body of Christ, carry out their own and proper roles within the
liturgical assembly (see STL 10).[10] This Body of Christ, the ordained
and the baptized, are gathered in Christ to worship the Father
through the saving Work of the Son in the Holy Spirit. This gathering in Christ is foundational, if you will, for understanding liturgical
participation and, as such, underscores all levels and types of participation and shapes them. We are called as those baptized into the
saving Mystery of Christ, especially at the Sunday Eucharist, to enter
into this Mystery, to enter with Christ the Lord by the power of his
Holy Spirit into the worship of God the Father (see STL 12).

The first level of participation can be described as an internal
or interior awareness and engagement of the Sacred Mysteries celebrated in the Liturgy. Only with an internal engagement of the Sacred
Mysteries, a union of self with the members of the Church in the
paschal offering of the Lord, does a second level of participation,
described as an external participation, receive its meaning and achieve
its purpose. External participation, again on the part of all the
ordained and the baptized, expresses and directs interior participation
in the worship of Almighty God (see STL 13).[11] In a profound way,
liturgical music serves the authentic participation more completely
than any of the other features or dimensions of the liturgical rites. To
allow liturgical music to assist with authentic participation is part of
the necessary work to be done.

Pastors and liturgical music ministers, mindful of their own
duty to participate internally and externally in the Sacred Liturgy,
have an important task of instructing the faithful to see that liturgical
music serves both levels of participation. We all listen to the words
sung and are shaped by them. Our listening during the course of the
Sacred Liturgy is more than simply hearing. It is also an invitation
to unite ourselves to what we hear so to lift our mind and soul in the
worship of God. Then, in the plan and choice for liturgical music,
everyone—the ordained and the baptized—are expected to sing, and

---

10. See SC 28; see also GIRM 91.

11. See SC 52 and 64 for helpful insights into internal and external participation in the Sacred
Liturgy.

sing well, the dialogues, the very texts of the liturgy and the processional chants to express this union of mind and soul with everyone
else gathered in Christ to worship the Father. *Sing to the Lord* rightfully acknowledges that our participation in the Liturgy is challenging
(see STL 14). However, every effort should be expended for authentic
participation as part of the fruit of the renewal of the rites of the
Sacred Liturgy, especially by singing the Liturgy, so that God is truly
glorified and, in doing so, his people have a share in his holiness.

Conclusion

We have discussed some of the theological foundations proposed by
Sing to the Lord for the very important purpose of orienting a discussion of liturgical music in the celebration of the Sacred Liturgy itself,
which is the purpose of this book. Answers in this chapter to questions about why we sing the Liturgy and how singing leads to more
complete participation in the Mystery of Christ now takes us to the
next step, examining the expectation of the members of the Church
to sing the Liturgy. The next chapter will also consider the important
topics in *Sing to the Lord* on singing with regard to leadership
and formation of liturgical music ministers, including in the Catholic
school, diverse cultures and languages, and singing in Latin.

Chapter 2

The Singers of Liturgical Music

INTRODUCTION

This chapter builds on the previous chapter's theological responses to why we sing the Liturgy and how this singing aids liturgical participation. We will describe the roles and duties of all the members of the Church—the ordained and baptized—to sing the Mysteries of Christ. Particular attention will be given to those among the baptized who assume leadership and responsibility in liturgical music ministry. The contemporary issues of diverse cultures and languages and the celebration of the Liturgy, including the singing of Latin, will also be addressed.

FORMATION REQUIREMENTS

The ordained, above all because of their sacramental leadership roles in the liturgical assembly, bear the weight and duty of fostering the tradition and practice of singing the Sacred Liturgy. Among all of the possibilities for the Bishop, priests, and deacons to help promote the practice of singing the Liturgy is simply to sing, both what is proper to their role in the liturgical rites and with the people. The liturgical assembly and the liturgical musicians among them share in a certain way a similar duty of fostering the tradition and practice of singing the Sacred Liturgy, especially the leaders in liturgical musical roles. All sing in response to the Bishop, the priests, and deacons and sing with them.

Formation and Duties of the Ordained

Sing to the Lord rightly presents the significance of the formation and duties of the Bishop, priests, and deacons for singing in the course of the celebrations of the liturgical rites (see STL 16–22).

The Bishop carries the responsibility as moderator of the Sacred Liturgy to promote authentic liturgical music.[1] In summary, *Sing to the Lord* describes the role of the Bishop to be a promoter by his own good example, by encouraging sung participation, by attending to the practice of liturgical music both in his cathedral and the parish churches, by arranging for the continued musical education of clergy and liturgical musicians, and also by the liturgical musical training of future priests and deacons (see STL 16).

In a practical and professional way the Bishop is assisted in his duties to promote authentic liturgical music through the services of the diocesan Office for Worship and the diocesan liturgical or liturgical music commission (see STL 17).

The priest, similar to the Bishop himself for the diocese, bears the responsibility to promote authentic liturgical music in the parish and especially with those entrusted with leadership in liturgical music. Good example is essential: "The importance of the priest's participation in the Liturgy, especially by singing, cannot be overemphasized" (STL 19). The priest sings the dialogues and the people respond and he sings with the people the parts that belong to both priest and people (see STL 19). It is true that some priests cannot sing the liturgical texts in a suitable voice. This does not diminish their responsibility to declaim these same texts in a dignified and respectable manner. Moreover, a priest should not sing simply for his own convenience (see STL 19).

More and more priests will be assisted in their responsibility to sing the Liturgy with programs of priestly formation that make it a priority to train priests to do so with particular emphasis on chanting those parts of the Mass belonging to the priest celebrant, especially the dialogues, the presidential prayers, and the Eucharistic Prayer (see STL 20). The priest sings with the people the parts of the Mass that belong to them in common. The priest does not sing the parts that belong to the people alone, such as their responses to his

---

1. See GIRM 22.

dialogues including the response to the Mystery of Faith (see STL 21). This obviously respects the integrity of the liturgical dialogue.

The deacon, especially in his guiding role of directing the baptized in the celebration of the Sacred Liturgy, serves them well by his own example (see STL 22). The deacon should be prepared to sing the dialogues, texts, and liturgical invitations that are proper to him as well as the various litanies in the different rites. Deacons should be trained to sing the Gospel on occasion and the *Exultet* at the Easter Vigil (see STL 23).

Serious and comprehensive liturgical musical formation of the clergy must combine with good practical example on their part to promote the sung celebration of the Sacred Liturgy. Bishops, priests, and deacons must know why they sing, what they sing, how to sing, and, above all, sing. In this way documents like *Sing to the Lord* will have the expected impact on the liturgical life of the Church in the United States. Ongoing formation programs in liturgical music at the diocesan level seem like a fine encouragement for clergy to sing and sing well the Sacred Liturgy. In this way, clergy, whether by programs or workshops on liturgical singing or by personal study of the topic, will guide and lead the faithful to sing the Sacred Liturgy.

Formation and Duties of the Liturgical Assembly

All participate in the divine event of the Sacred Liturgy according to their order in the Church. After examining the participation of the ordained, we now will consider the participation of the faithful. The faithful, the baptized members of the liturgical assembly, participate first of all by the offering of themselves in the Sacrifice of Christ that occurs most excellently in the Eucharist, as well as in all of the liturgical celebrations. This offering of self is known as actual or active participation (see STL 24). Singing expresses this actual participation. Keeping in mind all that was said in the last chapter on why we sing, the Bishops' declare that "Singing is one of the primary ways that the assembly of the faithful participates actively in the Liturgy. . . . The musical formation of the assembly must be a continuing concern in order to foster full, conscious, and active participation" (STL 26).

The faithful need to be informed as to why they sing the Sacred Liturgy and that it is the Liturgy itself that should be sung, the very texts themselves. The faithful need to be instructed by their pastors and liturgical music ministers that singing the Sacred Liturgy strengthens faith and occasions a sacramental encounter with the Mysteries of Christ. The formation of the faithful also includes a review of liturgical music and a wide experience of its many forms. In *Sing to the Lord*, the Bishops recommend a familiarity with a stable repertoire of liturgical songs rich in theological content to deepen the faith of the community especially through repetition and memorization (see STL 27). Sometimes, it can be too easy to underestimate both the capacity of the person in the pew to appreciate what is liturgical music and their desire to sing it. Exposure to liturgical music over time accompanied by clear catechesis goes a long way to make singing liturgical music more of the norm.

It is from the members of the liturgical assembly that the roles of choir member, psalmist, cantor, organist, and other instrumentalists emerge for their service of the Sacred Liturgy.

Formation and Duties of the Liturgical Music Ministers

Sing to the Lord provides a listing of the various liturgical music ministries and a description of their duties. This listing and description combines to show how the liturgical music ministries support singing the Sacred Liturgy and properly guide singing of the liturgical assembly. In fact, all of the liturgical music ministries serve to enhance the liturgical singing of all those assembled to celebrate the Sacred Liturgy. The singing liturgical assembly is the image of the heavenly assembly. This is why *Sing to the Lord* describes the singing of the faithful as "the primary song of the Liturgy" (see STL 28).

The importance of the liturgical choir cannot be underestimated for its unique role in assisting the whole liturgical assembly in sung worship. The choir supports the singing of the liturgical assembly, responds with the faithful to the dialogues of the celebrant, alternates in the singing of litanies, and at times sings alone. "[The choir is] able to enrich the celebration by adding musical elements beyond the capabilities of the congregation alone" (STL 28). However, the choir should never see itself as performing for the

liturgical assembly or taking its place but aiding in the worship of
God (see STL 29–32).[2] The Bishops in *Sing to the Lord* emphasize
the need, importance, and role of the choir today which agrees with
the instruction provided in the *Constitution on the Sacred Liturgy*.[3]
Choir members should possess the requisite skills for the musical
tasks and an understanding of liturgical music, and acknowledge their
role in the celebrations (see STL 28).

The psalmist is the one who announces in song the biblical
response to the first reading and, at times, sings the verse during the
Gospel acclamation.[4] The liturgical role of the psalmist as a pro-
claimer of the word of God should be distinguished from the cantor,
a leader of song. The psalmist, like the lector, should possess pronunciation skills and understand the nuances of the text. Typically
the psalmist sings the Responsorial Psalm from the ambo (see
STL 34–36).[5]

The cantor is especially helpful when no choir is present to
carry out the role of supporting the singing of the liturgical assembly.
Sing to the Lord specifically details some of the duties of the cantor:
to sing the *Kyrie* or the invocations of the third form of the Penitential
Act; to chant the acclamations after the biblical readings except the
Gospel; to sing the verse before the Gospel; to sing the petitions
of the Prayer of the Faithful and to lead the Lamb of God. The cantor
can also intone the *Gloria* and the *Alleluia* as well as sing the psalm
verses to the processional chants at the Entrance, Offertory, and
Communion. If necessary, the cantor can assume the role of psalmist,
although as already mentioned it is a distinct liturgical music ministry
(see STL 34, 37).[6]

The presence of a cantor is the typical practice for the sung
celebration of the Sacred Liturgy. *Sing to the Lord* collects some very
important guiding points for this ministry to enhance both the work
of the cantor and the dignity of the celebration itself. The cantor

---

2. The unique role of the choir singing certain parts of the celebration of the Sacred Liturgy
is explained in more detail in Part III of this book.

3. See SC 114 in part.

4. See GIRM 129; see also LFM 56.

5. See GIRM 61, 309.

6. While it is possible for the cantor to sing many of the parts that properly belong to the
priest or deacon, choir or psalmist, this occurs only in the true absence or possibility of such parts
being intoned or sung by the proper minister.

should take part in the singing of the liturgical assembly when the body sings together and be mindful of blending his/her voice with the whole group. Overall, the cantor should be more recessive in singing with the whole liturgical assembly, use clear and modest invitational gestures, and assume a place, other than the ambo, that does not distract from the principal liturgical action (see STL 38–40).[7] The cantor is not a performer for the liturgical assembly but rather guides and leads its singing.

Instrumentalists, especially the organist, are the true leaders of song for the liturgical assembly and assist the music ministers throughout the course of the celebration of the Sacred Liturgy (see STL 41). They are the true leaders in as much as they prompt and promote the actual singing of the Sacred Liturgy. Instrumentalists provide an additional and powerful sound dimension intended to help convey the meaning of the sung texts. As with all the ministers of liturgical music, the requisite skill and its maintenance, knowledge of the liturgical rites, and the proper spiritual disposition to engage in the celebration of the Mysteries belongs to the list of their duties.

Properly, all music ministers taking part in the celebration of the Sacred Liturgy, as with all liturgical ministers, should be Roman Catholic and, during Mass, bring their service to completion with Eucharistic Communion. This presumption does not represent any prejudice against those musicians who are not Roman Catholic, rather, it accords the same parallel understanding of liturgical ministry for a music minister with that of the lector or the server, for example. Typically, liturgical ministry arises from membership in the liturgical assembly and full participation in the liturgical action.

Finally, *Sing to the Lord* offers sound advice to the pastor regarding the assistance of a Director of Music Ministry. Over and above what can be said about the assistance such a director of music gives the pastor in the promotion of a sung celebration of the Sacred Liturgy (by employing the varied liturgical music ministries), this person must be properly trained and skilled in liturgical music. Even if this person is not a Roman Catholic, there is the same expectation for proper training and skill (see STL 45).

---

7. See LFM 33.

Vesture for liturgical music ministers

Sing to the Lord gives some advice concerning vesture for music ministers. In general, this document states that the music minister may dress in an alb or choir robe, or clean, presentable, modest clothing. Cassock and surplice, being clerical attire, are not recommended as vesture (see STL 33, 36, 40). There are a great variety of circumstances and situations where music ministers carry out their roles that this blanket suggestion fails to accommodate. Music ministers are indeed liturgical ministers and as such may wear an alb, yet there is a longstanding tradition of wearing both choir robes and, for men's choirs, cassocks and surplices. The pastor and liturgical musician might evaluate the circumstance and situation in light of what is both traditional and practical to the place and then make a local decision. In any case, a liturgical music minister never wears a stole or something similar to it since this vesture is reserved to the ordained. Whether or not the choice is made for liturgical music ministers to wear a particular vesture, it is a meaningful sign. Prescribed vesture identifies the specific liturgical role. No vesture identifies the association of the music minister with the liturgical assembly.

Finally, and a most important concluding point, something must be said about the faith life of all liturgical music ministers. Liturgical music ministers must be people of faith, faith in the Sacred Mysteries of the Lord celebrated in the Liturgy. This at once personal and corporate faith leads to a deeper interior level of participation in the Liturgy on the part of the liturgical music minister. It is this level of participation that leads liturgical music ministers, in their external participation, to be in service of the Liturgy itself and the liturgical assembly (see STL 32, 49).

LEADERSHIP AND FORMATION IN MUSIC MINISTRY AND CATHOLIC EDUCATION

Pastors are encouraged as they promote and support the sung celebration of the Sacred Liturgy to invite members of the faithful to assume liturgical musical leadership and guide their formation. In a general way, the pastor with the assistance of others should do this for the whole liturgical assembly. In a specific way, from among the faithful, people often emerge with skill and talent to carry out the duties of the various liturgical ministries described above (see STL 48). In *Sing to the Lord*, the Bishops identify some key elements to keep in mind when forming liturgical music ministers:

- an understanding that music ministers are indeed ministers who serve the Church at prayer through music and thus exercise a genuine liturgical ministry;
- they should be continuously formed to carry out their duties competently, which requires appropriate personal, spiritual, and professional formation;
- lastly, the liturgical music minister, if not a volunteer, deserves just compensation. He or she should have the necessary resources available to carry out his or her duties. (see STL 50–53.)

Adequate formation and resources for liturgical music ministers serve the overarching aim of the Bishops' document that the Sacred Liturgy is sung and done so for the glory of God and the benefit of all. This also is why Catholic schools and other institutions have a significant role in the formation of liturgical music ministers.

Catholic schools are a primary place to initiate young people into the leadership roles in liturgical music ministry and can be the beginning of proper formation for these roles. *Sing to the Lord* gives a broad and selective sweep to this topic (see STL 54–66). In doing so, the bishops echo the *Constitution on the Sacred Liturgy*:

> Great importance is to be attached to the teaching and practice of music in seminaries, in the novitiates and houses of study of religious of both sexes and also in Catholic institutions and schools. To impart this instruction, those in charge of teaching sacred music are to receive thourough training. It is recommended also that higher institutes of sacred music be established wherever possible whenever this can be done.
>
> Musicians and singers . . . must also be given a genuine liturgical training. (SC 115)

The proper and authentic liturgical musical formation of those who form others, especially in ministerial and instructional circumstances, is of paramount importance and must be a priority for the ongoing and consistent formation of the liturgical music ministers and the faithful. This type of formation promotes the understanding and practice of liturgical formation of all types as formation in what the

Church celebrates and believes with regard to the Sacred Mysteries of the Lord.

When the occasions arise, Catholic Schools and Catholic Religious Education programs must see the importance, both with teaching the faith and promoting liturgical music ministry, of having the authentic, worthy, and dignified celebrations of the Mysteries as a priority (see STL 54). In Catholic educational settings, students can receive a complete understanding of liturgical participation and become singers. This happens not only in the celebration of the Sacred Liturgy, but also with additional opportunities to sing from the liturgical repertoire. Singing in the Catholic schools promotes the various liturgical music ministries, especially choirs and cantors. The immediate aim of liturgical singing in the Catholic education setting, regardless of level, is to encourage the students to sing during the Sunday Eucharist (see STL 55). In fact, all liturgical efforts in the Catholic Schools or religious educational programs point to Sunday!

Catholic educational institutions serving adolescents and young adults should also provide education and formation in the Sacred Liturgy and liturgical music ministries according to the tradition and current liturgical norms of the Church. In this way, these same students are prepared to assume their rightful place in the Sunday liturgical assembly and in leadership roles in liturgical music ministries. In Catholic educational institutions, whether for children, adolescents, or young adults, the Sacred Liturgy must be celebrated according to the norms in the liturgical books and liturgical instructions (see STL 56). It is this practice, above all, that educates and forms students for true participation and future leadership roles in the Sacred Liturgy. Also, these same points should guide discussions of Masses for children, teens, and young adults, with regard to liturgical music. If what the Church expects in the celebration of the Sacred Liturgy is put aside in the preparation of these Mass, there is the real risk of compromising the communication of the faith as well as the formation in the faith.

Use of Other Vernacular Languages

In the United States today, it is possible to sing the Liturgy in a great variety of languages. Singing the Sacred Liturgy in the vernacular also brings to the celebration the cultural context of the sung language, which impacts the expression of the faith. While, on the one hand, there must always be a consideration for the culture of the constituents of the liturgical assembly, this consideration is at the service of the authentic celebration of the Mysteries.[8]

In *Sing to the Lord*, the Bishops encourage the fostering of cultural and ethnic diversity and the new richness this brings to the celebration of the Liturgy (see STL 57–60). Multilingual and multicultural celebrations of the Sacred Liturgy require guidelines so that whatever linguistic or cultural decisions are made with regard to the celebration are in harmony with the theological and liturgical meaning of the rites (see STL 60). No single culture has the right to refashion and reinterpret the Sacred Mysteries to suit an individual context. A necessary aspect of attention to the use of other languages in the celebration of the Liturgy and inclusiveness of culture is the outreach to immigrants who have a home in the celebration of the faith (see STL 58). Above all, the use of other languages and the introduction of features of different cultures as a type of tokenism must be avoided (see STL 60). It would be inappropriate to simply employ the use of another language or cultural feature for its own sake when it would neither serve the Liturgy nor the assembly.

More and more in the United States, a multilingual and multicultural country, we need to provide for singing the Sacred Liturgy with due regard for both of these dimensions. It is not enough for us to simply sing one or two hymns in another language or introduce an ethnic character to the celebration. Rather, planning and preparing for multilingual and multicultural celebrations requires a careful integration of language and culture within the given framework of what is already and always directed for the authentic celebration of the Mysteries of the Lord. It must be remembered that in every language and cultural context, God is the one at work in

---

8. This discussion of culture and language and the celebration of the Sacred Liturgy benefits from a reading of the 1994 document of the Congregation for Divine Worship and the Discipline of the Sacraments, *Inculturation and the Roman Liturgy*.

celebration of the Sacred Liturgy and that the Mystery is not the work of human hands.

Use of Latin in Liturgical Music

An increasingly relevant topic with regard to liturgical music is singing Latin liturgical music. Although the topic is timely, especially because it is addressed more and more in papal exhortations and magisterial documents, it meets with a diverse set of responses and practices. The celebration of the Sacred Liturgy in the vernacular is the norm, most especially in the United States (see STL 61). Parishes throughout the country carry out the rites in a long list of approved liturgical languages with the necessary approved liturgical books. However, it is possible to sing in Latin in addition to the vernacular in the same celebration.

Pastors are encouraged by the Bishops in *Sing to the Lord* to foster the role of Latin in the Liturgy (see STL 61, 74). This mandate includes a history of similar directives to pastors since the Second Vatican Council.[9] A good question is why. The singing of the Latin Proper and hymnody, and the Latin Ordinary of the Mass and the Creed and the Our Father allow for modern day liturgical assemblies to sing the Mysteries in a language in which the faith was conceived, celebrated, and taught for centuries. It is the language of generations of believers who have brought us to this day. The singing of Latin allows for a more precise and consistent expression of the faith in the way the whole Church celebrates and teaches the faith, which is the same faith now also contained in its vernacular rendition. Singing in Latin joins the members of many parts and places of the Church throughout the world into a unity of worship (see STL 62). Singing in Latin affords the modern day liturgical assembly the opportunity to receive and experience the living worship of the Church and the richness of her liturgical patrimony and the cultural patrimony of the Roman Rite.

The use of Latin in the singing of the Sacred Liturgy calls for an objective criterion on the part of the pastor and the liturgical music minister. A part of this criterion as identified in *Sing to the Lord* is

---

9. For example, see GIRM 41; and SCar 62.

that singers must be competent in Latin pronunciation and in understanding its meaning (see STL 63). The plan to sing in Latin should
refer to those parts recommended by the Church today: the Ordinary,
the Proper, and hymnody (see STL 75). Additionally, the liturgical
assembly needs to be prepared in order to sing properly in Latin.
This preparation includes aids for singing and translation. The use
of Latin may diminish participation if its reintroduction fails to
consider all that is necessary to assist the liturgical assembly to sing
and listen.

Conclusion

The priority of liturgical music formation of both the ordained and
the baptized, and especially of the liturgical music ministers, must be
honored with sound, concrete, and practical measures to make sure
that our liturgical song is a truly song unto the Lord. Solid liturgical
music formation will make sure that our song leads us to engage
the Mysteries of Christ for the praise of God and for our growth in
holiness and service. We briefly and carefully noted the requirements
of liturgical music formation, and paid special attention to diverse
cultural circumstances and the use of several languages, including the
language of the Roman Liturgy. In the next Chapter we will consider
several dimensions of music for the Sacred Liturgy, its instrumentation, and related requirements.

Chapter 3

Expression of Liturgical Music

Introduction

In this chapter we will look carefully at what the Bishops have to say about the qualities of liturgical music, including current incentives to sing Gregorian chant and encouragement for suitable compositions in the vernacular. We will also discuss the great variety of instruments to support liturgical singing, as well as several related topics that promote liturgical singing.

Qualities of Liturgical Music

In *Sing to the Lord*, the Bishops outline the dimensions of liturgical music according to three principal guiding factors: the ritual dimension, the spiritual dimension, and the cultural context. A principle from the Second Vatican Council is recalled as the overarching criterion for these guiding factors.

The *Constitution on the Sacred Liturgy* states:

> [s]acred music will be the more holy the more closely it is joined to the liturgical rite, whether by adding delight to prayer, fostering oneness of spirit, or investing the rites with greater solemnity upon the sacred rites. (SC 112)

Perhaps the word "holy" in this principle might sound too ambiguous or somewhat vague as a category to describe the quality of sacred or liturgical music. The use of this word, however, immediately points to the Holy One, to God. The aim of this principle is to grasp the multifaceted capacity of liturgical music, a text and sound which relates to the worship of God. Liturgical music does just this when it immediately suggests that it is "pleasing"; and when it unites worshippers together, and gives a dignified expression to the carrying out of the rites. This all may sound quite subjective even as a principle. However, *Sing to the Lord* further develops this concept of "holiness" when it describes the ritual and spiritual dimensions of liturgical music as well as its cultural context.

The ritual dimension sees the music that accompanies a rite as both serving and expressing the rite itself, that is, connected to the liturgical action. Thus, the music should be suited to the structure of the rite and illustrate its meaning as sung by the priest and people. The texts, and often the notations for this ritual music, can be found in the liturgical books in place or in an appendix (see STL 68).

The spiritual dimension acknowledges the music as it explicates the theological meaning of the rite and draws attention to how the rite manifests God's saving work and action in liturgical celebrations. This spiritual dimension also joins together those singing and listening into a communion of prayer and praise arising from the authentic sense of the rite (see STL 69).

The cultural context sees the music in the actual measurable setting of the celebration of the Sacred Liturgy, for example, the nature of those assembled, their ethnicity, and the place. Sometimes the Sacred Liturgy is celebrated within a broad cultural context that can be difficult to define. The ritual and spiritual dimensions of liturgical music should not be diminished in favor of highlighting the cultural context. Rather, the cultural context, while it impacts the promotion of these dimensions, is served by the ritual and spiritual dimensions (see STL 70).

With all this being said, the Church in her liturgical books provides texts and notations for singing the Liturgy. The use of these given texts and notations above all promote the "holiness" of liturgical music and serve the inherent ritual and spiritual dimensions in a favorable way and enliven the cultural context with an authentic celebration. It is also important for the pastor and the liturgical music minister to look to the Church's treasury of liturgical music and the vernacular music inspired by it (see STL 71).

The Use of Gregorian Chant

The following statement in the *Constitution on the Sacred Liturgy* finds regular repetition in the instructions on music and the liturgy since the Second Vatican Council:

> The Church acknowledges Gregorian chant as specially suited to the Roman liturgy; therefore, other things being equal, it should be given pride of place in liturgical services (SC 116).

The *General Instruction of the Roman Missal* repeats and develops the same point:

> All other things being equal, Gregorian chant holds pride of place because it is proper to the Roman Liturgy. Other types of sacred music, in particular polyphony, are in no way excluded, provided they correspond to the spirit of the liturgical action and that they foster the participation of all the faithful.
>
> Since faithful from different countries come together ever more frequently, it is fitting that they know how to sing together at least some parts of the Ordinary of the Mass in Latin, especially the Creed and the Lord's Prayer, set to the simpler melodies. (GIRM 41)

The U.S. Bishops repeat the statement of the Council and recall that Gregorian chant forms a living connection with the past and is the traditional music of the Roman Rite and, as such, forms a link with the whole Church (see STL 72). Its use today, according to the authors of *Sing to the Lord* and as suggested by the Missal instruction above, requires the pastor and the liturgical music minister to ensure participation of those who sing and listen (see STL 73).

There is another point, and perhaps the more noteworthy liturgical point, with regard to Gregorian chant: It is "proper" to the Roman Rite. Gregorian chant, in addition to its praiseworthiness from an historical, musical, and universal perspective, works as music and rite are intended to work together. The text and sound of the music serve the rites in terms of their nature and meaning—the ritual and spiritual dimensions—and enjoy great availability to the multiplicity of cultural contexts. In this sense, Gregorian chant possesses a very high quality as liturgical music. It fits the description of "holy" as identified by the *Constitution on the Sacred Liturgy*.

The Church, through the work and assistance of the monks of Solemnes, has made available a large collection of the Latin chants for use with the celebration of the modern Roman Rite.[1] Pastors and liturgical music ministers would want to have on hand the *Graduale Romanum* and the *Graduale Simplex* (see STL 76). Both of these song books contain the propers and suggested chants for the Entrance, Offertory, and Communion listed in the options for these parts of the Mass in the *General Instruction of the Roman Missal*. Use of the chants in these books demonstrates what is "proper" about Gregorian chant, which is the seamless connection between song and action. In fact, the song insinuates itself with the action and becomes a feature of it. It is this aspect of the property of Gregorian chant, which includes its sound, that is expected to influence chanting in the vernacular.[2] This concept of music corresponding to the liturgical action, as noted above in the *General Instruction of the Roman Missal*, belongs to the quality of all music used in the celebration of the Sacred Liturgy.

The *General Instruction of the Roman Missal* suggests, for the sake of international unity, that at least the Ordinary of the Mass should be known and sung in Latin as well as simpler settings of the Creed and the Lord's Prayer. Pope Paul VI published a small leaflet of Gregorian chant, Jubilate Deo, in the early days of the vernacular celebration of the Mass.[3] In fact, Pope Benedict XVI's exhortation *Sacramentum caritatis* takes the *General Instruction* even further when he encourages the singing of the Gregorian chant in its own right.[4]

The adaptation of the U.S. Bishops to the *General Instruction of the Roman Missal*, which lists as the first option for the singing of the processional chants of the Mass according to the proper in the *Graduale Romanum* or the *Graduale Simplex*, additionally expects pastors and liturgical musicians to consider this possibility (see STL 76). To date there are no authoritative translations of the *Graduale Romanum* or the *Graduale Simplex*. When they are employed as

---

1. Sacrosanctum Concilium, 117, promoted these musical books, "The typical edition of the books of Gregorian chant is to be completed, and a more critical edition is to be prepared of those books already published since the restoration by St. Pius X. It is desirable also that an edition be prepared containing simpler melodies for use in small churches."

2. John Paul II, Chirograph, 12.

3. See Letter to the Bishops or the Minimum Repertoire of Plain chant, *Voluntati Obsequeas*, Sacred Congregation for Divine Worship, April 14, 1974 in Notitiae, April 1974, p. 123-126.

4. SCar, 42.

options, both aids to participation, and translations are in order (see STL 76). The modern liturgical assembly is entitled to benefit from the rich patrimony of the Church's musical tradition as well as the "proper" music of the Roman Rite.

VERNACULAR LITURGICAL MUSIC

The celebration of the Sacred Mysteries in the vernacular has introduced new and wonderful possibilities for singing these same Mysteries in the vernacular as well. Countless efforts mark the years of singing in the vernacular with both chants and hymnody, some quite positive and others not so. As in the past, as indicated by *Sing to the Lord* (see STL 81–82), the Church continues to be in need of musicians and artists to craft new melodies to suit the celebration of the modern liturgical rites, always keeping in mind the "holiness" of this music and its appropriateness to the liturgical rites. The traditional sound should inspire the contemporary sound as part of the audible translation of texts intended to be sung. The genius of an age and culture can only add to the authenticity of new compositions when the intent of the liturgical celebration is served over and above anything else. An important assessment of suitability of a new composition as well as its inspired sound from the tradition is doctrinal integrity (see STL 83). Liturgical music expresses and forms the faith of those who sing and listen. Modern composers, when writing to accompany texts other than those found in the Sacred Scriptures and the liturgical books, must be disciples of the Creed and allow their new work to profess the faith of the Church.[5] Any new liturgical compositions for use in the Sacred Liturgy require the approval of the Bishops through the USCCB Secretariat for Divine Worship (see STL 108–109).[6]

THE USE OF INSTRUMENTS

The U.S. Bishops highlight the human voice above all other instruments (see STL 86). Yes, this is the first instrument in the sung

---

5. See SC, 121.

6. See Bishops' Committee on the Liturgy (BCL), Policy for the Approval of Musical Compositions for the Liturgy, November 10, 1996. BCC Newsletter Volume XXXIII, Jan/Feb 1997.

celebration of the Sacred Liturgy. It is the voice that mediates the word and works of God as the Mysteries unfold within the rites of the Church. To sing well, to proclaim well, to speak well in the course of the Liturgy is to enhance our personal and corporate participation in the celebration of God's Work, our redemption. Singing without accompaniment is to be encouraged to promote a more spontaneous singing of the Sacred Liturgy in small settings or settings without the benefit of instrumentation.

The *Constitution on the Sacred Liturgy* assigns the organ a special ranking among other instruments in the service of the Roman Rite and also speaks of the use of other instruments:

> In the Latin Church the pipe organ is to be held in high esteem, for it is the traditional musical instrument that adds a wonderful splendor to the Church's ceremonies and powerfully lifts up man's mind to God and to higher things.
>
> But other instruments also may be admitted for use in divine worship with the knowledge and consent of the competent territorial authority . . . .This applies, however, only on the condition that the instruments are suitable or can be made suitable, for sacred use, are in accord with the dignity of the place of worship and truly contribute to the uplifting of the faithful. (SC 120)

While the organ enjoys a high rank in the liturgical musical tradition of the Church, it is clear from the *Constitution on the Sacred Liturgy* that it is not the only instrument permitted for use in the celebration of the Sacred Liturgy. The *General Instruction of the Roman Missal* reiterates what is set forth in the *Constitution on the Sacred Liturgy* with regard to the organ and other instruments.[7]

The pipe organ and many electronic organs as well have a capacity to sustain the singing of large groups of people in large spaces and to provide a variety of sounds to accommodate the many different meanings of the rites of the Liturgy (see STL 87–88). Presently, there is no restrictive legislation for the United States on the use of different instruments in the celebration of the Liturgy. In fact, it is quite common for a variety of instruments in addition to the organ to be used to accompany song during the Sacred Liturgy. If there is any

---

7. See GIRM 393.

restriction, it is found in assessing an instrument's suitability in terms of its contribution to the "holiness" of the music (see STL 90).

Instrumental music, derived from the tradition and compatible with the liturgical action, has a place in the course of the celebration, especially when no text or music is prescribed to accompany a rite. An example of this is the preparation of the altar and the gifts during the Mass (see STL 44, 174). Certainly, instrumental music can serve to prepare those assembled for the Liturgy beforehand and to conclude liturgical celebrations. "Instrumentalists are encouraged to play pieces from the treasury of sacred music by composers of various eras and cultures."[8] Even instrumental music, especially when it is improvised, should be carried out with a sense of "holiness" (see STL 43, 92).

Recorded music should not be used in the celebration of the Sacred Liturgy according to *Sing to the Lord* (see STL 93–94). It is not the voice of the believer, the voice of the worshiper and, as such, is always inappropriate in the course of the celebration of the Eucharist, the other Sacraments and the Liturgy of the Hours. Recorded music certainly can serve as an aid to learning music. Even in cases identified in *Sing to the Lord* when recorded music seems advisable, like outdoor processions, every effort should be made to actually sing in those circumstances (see STL 94). The recommendation in *Sing to the Lord* for recorded music to "fill in" for periods of silence during some of the sacramental rites fails to recognize the actual communal participation of the faithful in the Liturgy with a corporate act of silence (see STL 94).

The U.S. Bishops in *Sing to the Lord* offer sound advice on the location of musicians and their instruments. Musicians and instruments for the Sacred Liturgy should be located in a place to serve the whole liturgical assembly. There are two points to keep in mind:
- the liturgical musicians are members of the faithful and their place is near to or related to that of the liturgical assembly; and
- the musicians themselves are participants in the liturgical celebration so their location should assist this (see STL 95–96).

The choir should easily seem a part of the liturgical assembly (see STL 98). This does not rule out the use of a choir loft. The psalmist

---

8. STL 91.

should easily be able to assume the ambo for the Responsorial Psalm (see STL 97). The cantor or leader of song should be able to move easily to the front of the liturgical assembly to lead song. Liturgical music ministers should not take their place in the sanctuary (see STL 97).

The U.S. Bishops address important lateral topics that, when in place, promote and ensure the efforts of well chosen liturgical music, well prepared liturgical music ministers, appropriate instrumentation, suitable acoustics (see STL 101–104), copyright and reprint norms, as well as participation aids (see STL 105–107). The United States Conference of Catholic Bishops has previously issued guidelines that are also helpful on these topics.[9]

The pastor and liturgical music minister, as part of their responsibility to both singing the Sacred Liturgy and to those who will sing and listen, should pay careful attention to the maintenance of liturgical instruments as well as the conduciveness of the room and materials for high quality sound and singing.

CONCLUSION

This chapter concludes Part I of this book. We have covered the quality of liturgical music (including the singing of Gregorian chant), instrumentation, and the conciliar concept of "holiness" and liturgical music. This determination of holiness involves consideration of the ritual and spiritual dimensions, as well as an awareness of the cultural context of the music. In all of its various expressions, the "holiness" of all aspects of liturgical music will greatly promote a sense of all the qualities of liturgical music with renewed attention to its sound and texts. Liturgical music distinguishes itself from the large treasury of sacred music, both in the Roman Catholic tradition and in other traditions. Liturgical music also distinguishes itself from popular and devotional religious music, again among Roman Catholics and other Christian communions. This distinction of what constitutes liturgical music—that the texts and music arrive from the actual celebration of the Sacred Liturgy—establishes a hierarchy among liturgical music,

---

9. See USCCB, *Built of Living Stones: Art, Architecture and Worship* (BCL) (Washington, DC: USCCB, 2000), *Guidelines for the Publications of Participation Aids, June 17, 1998. BCC Newsletter Volume XXXIV, July/August 1998.*

sacred music, and religious music. In the recent past, these three types of music have often been used without discrimination in actual celebrations. *Sing to the Lord*, with its emphasis on a theological purpose to singing, a purpose leading to actual participation, guided by the clergy and faithful, especially liturgical music ministers, promotes in the first place the use of liturgical music. In Part II, we will take a look at "Liturgical Music: Patterns and Choices." We will examine how liturgical music is planned according to what is sung and discuss the selection of appropriate liturgical music.

Part II

Liturgical Music: Patterns and Choices

Liturgical music has its own logic for answering the questions of how it is prepared, as well as how to determine the quality of the music for the sung parts of the liturgical rites. In the reformed rites of the Roman Rite, it is expected that the Sacred Liturgy be sung. There is an inherent schema or pattern for when and what to sing (see STL 110). In Chapters 4 and 5 we outline the principles for recognizing this pattern and the ways to choose the music for the sung parts of the liturgical rites.

Chapter 4

What is Progressive Solemnity?

INTRODUCTION

Many Catholics are still familiar with the term "High Mass" which was a popular way in the past of describing a celebration of the Sacred Liturgy with song and additional ceremony. In fact, in the past there were specific title designations for the various forms for the celebration of Mass with proper liturgical music, additional sacred ministers and rites. Although these designations no longer apply in the same way, the principle does still hold. In this chapter we will examine the principle of progressive solemnity, and provide a helpful tool to use when preparing liturgical celebrations.

THE PRINCIPLE OF PROGRESSIVE SOLEMNITY

Certain liturgical times and occasions expect a solemn celebration of the Sacred Liturgy and others a not-so-solemn celebration. The Holy Days of Easter and Christmas, because of the Mysteries they celebrate, certainly expect a more solemn celebration than weekdays of Ordinary Time. And the fact that the Liturgy is typically a sung celebration, with singing as the normative way to celebrate, guiding principles are needed to promote more solemn celebrations as well as to provide for suitable daily celebrations. Thus, there is the need today for the principle of progressive solemnity.

 While progressive solemnity takes into account all the features of a celebration, including ceremony and the appointments where the Liturgy occurs, our concern here is with the ordering of liturgical music. This ordering of liturgical music ranges from an occasion when everything is sung to when nothing at all is sung. This contemporary understanding of progressive solemnity is first described for singing the reformed rites in the introductory material to the Liturgy of the Hours (see STL 111).[1] Again, we sing in order to strengthen the expression of the faith the Liturgy celebrates and on occasion the Church asks for a more heightened sacramental encounter with the Mystery the Liturgy celebrates. This is why there are occasions when more is sung than other times and days.

When applying the principle of progressive solemnity with its plan for several intermediate stages of singing liturgical music, we first need to consider the liturgical day or occasion. The Liturgical Year itself identifies days and seasons which in themselves are solemn celebrations of the Mysteries of the Lord and as such call for sung solemn celebrations of the Sacred Liturgy. We immediately think of the Sacred Easter Triduum, Sundays and Solemnities and the Easter Season. On these days and occasions, there is much singing of the Liturgy itself. Other days during the Liturgical Year do not carry the same solemn weight like the weekdays of Ordinary Time and the memorials of the saints. And on these days, there may be very little singing of the Liturgy itself.[2]

The character of each of the elements of the Sacred Liturgy is the next important consideration, with some of these always calling for singing and others only on the most solemn of occasions (see STL 112). The size and musical capacity of the liturgical assembly should be another consideration, as well as the available liturgical musical resources. The combination of all of these dimensions of the liturgical celebration should figure into the application of the principle of progressive solemnity. The consistent use of this same principle will then promote the singing of the Sacred Liturgy as normative.

PROGRESSIVE SOLEMNITY IN *MUSICAM SACRAM*

During the period of the reform of the rites of the Sacred Liturgy following the Second Vatican Council, the 1967 Roman document *Musicam sacram* proposed an initial paradigm of the principle of progressive solemnity, without calling it such, to promote an ordered singing of the Sacred Liturgy.

---

1. See GILOH 273.
2. See STL 116 for a proposed pattern for singing at daily Mass.

Musicam sacram identifies various stages of singing the Mass in terms of degrees. A review of this paradigm is helpful at this point.

These degrees are so arranged that the first may be used even by itself, but the second and third, wholly or partially, may never be used without the first. In this way the faithful will be continually led toward an ever greater participation in the singing.

The following belong to the first degree:

(a) In the entrance rites: the greeting of the priest together with the reply of the people; the prayer.

(b) In the Liturgy of the Word: the acclamations at the Gospel.

(c) In the Eucharistic Liturgy: the prayer over the offerings; the preface with its dialogue and the *Sanctus*; the final doxology of the Canon, the Lord's Prayer with its introduction and embolism; the *Pax Domini*; the prayer after the Communion; the formulas of dismissal.

The following belong to the second degree:

(a) the *Kyrie, Gloria* and *Agnus Dei*;

(b) the Creed;

(c) the prayer of the faithful.

The following belong to the third degree:

(a) the songs at the Entrance and Communion processions;

(b) the songs after the Lesson or Epistle;

(c) the Alleluia before the Gospel;

(d) the song at the Offertory;

(e) the readings of Sacred Scripture, unless it seems more suitable to proclaim them without singing. (MS 28-31)

A careful reading of these three degrees outlined in *Musicam sacram* illustrates a plan for progressive solemnity that considers the character of each of the elements of the Mass for singing. In the first degree, the dialogues and presidential prayers are sung above anything else. The elements listed in the first degree can be sung anytime and without those elements in the second or third degree being sung at all. Thus, these are the elements which have singing always attached to them. These elements would also have prescribed musical notations assigned to them in the *Roman Missal*; for example the introductory dialogues of the Preface.

In the second degree there are elements which could be described as independent rites or parts of the ordinary of the Mass. In the third degree are those elements which could be described as proper to the particular celebration of the Mass.

This glance at *Musicam sacram* helps us in its outline of degrees or stages for singing the Mass to apply the modern principle of progressive solemnity according to the nature of various sung elements of the liturgical rites. For example, in the first degree, we sing those elements that give expression to the assembled Church, the Body of Christ, celebrating the Mysteries of the Lord, that is, in the dialogues and the presidential prayers. Thus, the elements with the more significant theological liturgical meaning are sung first and then the singing of other elements follow. This, then, becomes the pattern for planning the sung elements of any celebration of the Sacred Liturgy.

A POSSIBLE PLAN FOR PROGRESSIVE SOLEMNITY

The current edition of the *General Instruction of the Roman Missal* echoes, although not exactly and not so precisely, the three degrees of *Musicam sacram* when it describes what should be sung at Mass in the current *Roman Missal*.

> Great importance should therefore be attached to the use of singing in the celebration of the Mass, with due consideration for the culture of the people and abilities of each liturgical assembly. Although it is not always necessary (e.g., in weekday Masses) to sing all the texts that are of themselves meant to be sung, every care should be taken that singing by the ministers and the people is not absent in celebrations that occur on Sundays and on holy days of obligation.

> In choosing the parts actually to be sung, however, preference should be given to those that are of greater importance and especially to those to be sung by the priest or the deacon or the lector, with the people responding, or by the priest and people together. (GIRM 40)

As with many Church documents that build on one another, the import of *Musicam sacram* finds its way into the *General Instruction* with its own directions for levels or degrees of singing during Mass depending on the time or occasion. The pastor and the liturgical music minister will see, in the review of the celebration of the Mass in Chapter 6 of this book, a more complete presentation of the sung options which orients a plan for progressive solemnity suitable for a particular place.

SOME SAMPLE PATTERNS FOR PROGRESSIVE SOLEMNITY

There is no universal plan for progressive solemnity. What we suggest are sample patterns for progressive solemnity according to the rank of liturgical celebrations, Sunday and Weekdays, Solemnities, Feasts and Memorials. These sample patterns follow the indicated levels of sung celebration identified in number forty of the *General Instruction of the Roman Missal* and the nature of the respective elements of the liturgical rites. The patterns that follow are for the celebration of the Eucharist and the Liturgy of the Hours. There is also a sample pattern for the chants that belong to the priest celebrant and the deacon.

Table 4.1   Sample Pattern for the Celebration of the Eucharist: Sundays, Weekdays, Solemnities, Feasts and Memorials

Mass	Sunday/ Solemnity	Feast	Weekday/ Memorial
Introductory Rites			
Entrance Chant	Sung	Sung	[Sung]
Greeting	Sung	sung	
Act of Penitence /Kyrie or Blessing, Sprinkling of Holy Water	Sung		
Gloria	Sung	Sung	
Collect	Sung	Sung	
Liturgy of the Word			
Responsorial Psalm	Sung	Sung	[Sung Response]
Chant before Gospel	Sung	Sung	[Sung]
Profession of Faith	[Sung]		
Prayer of the Faithful	[Sung]		
Liturgy of the Eucharist			
Offertory Chant	Sung/ Instrumental	Sung/ Instrumental	
Prayer over the Offerings	Sung	Sung	
Eucharistic Prayer	Sung	Sung	[Sung]
Lord's Prayer	Sung	Sung	
Rite of Peace	Sung		
Breaking of the Bread	Sung	Sung	[Sung]
Communion Chant	Sung	Sung	[Sung]
Hymn of Praise	Sung		
Prayer after Communion	Sung	Sung	
Concluding Rite			
Greeting/Blessing/Dismissal	Sung		
Hymn/Music after Mass	Sung/ Instrumental	Sung/ Instrumental	

Brackets[ ] Indicates the preferential option

Table 4.2   Sample Pattern for the Liturgy of the Hours: Morning and Evening Prayer Sundays, Weekdays, Solemnities, Feasts, and Memorials

Office	Sunday/Solemnity		Feast	Weekday/Memorial
	Morning/Evening Prayer II	Evening Prayer I		
Invitatory	Sung		Sung	Sung
Introduction	Sung	Sung	Sung	Sung
Hymn	Sung	Sung	Sung	Sung
Psalmody	Sung	Sung	Sung	Sung
Responsory	Sung	Sung	Sung	
Gospel Canticle	Sung	Sung	Sung	Sung
Intercessions	Sung			
Lord's Prayer	Sung	Sung	Sung	
Concluding Prayer	Sung	Sung	Sung	Sung
Greeting/Blessing/Dismissal	Sung	Sung	Sung	Sung

Table 4.3   Sample Pattern for Priest Celebrant Chants during the Celebration of the Eucharist

Part	Sunday Solemnity	Feast	Weekday Memorial
Sign of the Cross and Greeting	Sung	Sung	
Intone Gloria	If requested	If requested	
Collect	Sung	Sung	
Intone Creed	If requested		
Prayer of the Faithful	Sung		
Prayer over the Offerings	Sung	Sung	
Preface	Sung	Sung	
Anamnesis	Sung	Sung	Sung
Doxology	Sung	Sung	Sung
Lord's prayer	Sung	Sung	
Embolism	Sung	Sung	
Rite of Peace [with Greeting]	Sung		
Prayer after Communion	Sung	Sung	
Greeting and Blessing	Sung		

Table 4.4 Sample Pattern for the Deacon Chants during the Celebration of the Eucharist

Part	Sunday Solemnity	Feast	Weekday Memorial
Act of Penitence	If requested		
Gospel Introduction and Acclamation	Sung		
Invitation to the Sign of Peace	Sung		
Invitation to the Blessing	Sung		
Dismissal	Sung		

Table 4.5 Sample Pattern for the Celebrant Chants during the Liturgy of the Hours

Brackets[ ] indicates an option in the grid below.

Part	Sunday Solemnity	Feast	Weekday Memorial
Invitatory/Introduction	Sung	Sung	[Sung]
Intercessions	Sung		
Lord's Prayer	Sung	Sung	
Concluding Prayer	Sung	Sung	[Sung]
Greeting, Blessing, Dismissal	Sung	Sung	[Sung]

All of these sample patterns are just that, samples. We have assembled these patterns as guides for pastors and liturgical music ministers to craft their own based on the principle of progressive solemnity outlined above, the nature of the particular liturgical element to be sung, and the musical resources available. Above all, the patterns for progressive solemnity, which include the singing of the ordained and the faithful, if faithful to the levels for singing found in the *General Instruction*, will provide for an even and balanced sung celebration of the liturgical rites. Experimentation and flexibility are key features in the development of plans for progressive solemnity, along with a consistency as far as what should be sung. Such adjustments should not be arbitrary and should always be mindful why we sing the Sacred Liturgy.

Having reviewed the important principle of progressive solemnity, we are now ready to look at Chapter 5 with its description of what parts of the liturgical rites should be sung and the way to judge the quality of the music to be sung when preparing liturgical celebrations.

Chapter 5

What to Sing during the Sacred Liturgy

Introduction

In this chapter, we will consider what the Bishops' document says about the parts of the Sacred Liturgy to be sung, the importance of careful preparation, and the appropriate way to judge the quality of liturgical music. The way to judge liturgical music deserves special attention in terms of the previously described theological purpose behind singing the liturgy. We will also need to examine how singing the liturgy assists the liturgical assembly's engagement of the Mysteries of Christ.

What Are the Parts of the Liturgy to be Sung?

The aim of singing the celebration of the Sacred Liturgy requires a knowledge of the liturgical rites in their given parts and especially those parts which are rendered better when sung. The *General Instruction of the Roman Missal*, the *General Instruction of the Liturgy of the Hours* and the introductions to the other liturgical books, and most importantly, the rites themselves, should be the first resources that we consult when we want to know what parts of the liturgical celebration should typically be sung. In other words, the nature of these parts or texts suggests that they be sung rather than be recited.

First among these parts are the dialogues between the ordained and the faithful, other liturgical ministers and the faithful (see STL 115a). Singing these parts consistently puts into relief the solemn expression of the faith that the Sacred Liturgy is a celebration of the whole Christ, head and members. This is why the dialogues are always listed as first among the parts to be sung in a liturgical celebration in the liturgical documents. The *General Instruction* rightly says that the singing of the dialogues fosters and brings about communion between the priest and the people. (See GIRM 34.) Pastors and liturgical music ministers should make singing the dialogues a priority for themselves and in training the faithful in this practice.

Second, the acclamations, in a sense the spontaneous declarations of faith throughout the course of the liturgical rites, are to be sung again as an expression of the faith. These acclamations, for example during the Mass, include the lector's, "The word of the Lord," and the priest's, "Mystery of Faith," to which the faithful respond. *Sing to the Lord*, while highlighting the singing of acclamations, gives a mixed list of possible acclamations during the Eucharist, some of which are not acclamations properly speaking, such as, the *Sanctus* and the "Great Amen" (see STL 115a).[1]

Thirdly, in *Sing to the Lord*, the Bishops highlight the significance of the psalter as the songbook of the Liturgy (see STL 115b, 117). All throughout the course of the liturgical rites the psalms with antiphons properly fill out the processions and responses to the word of God and again, by their nature, should be sung (see STL 115b).[2]

Next, throughout the course of the liturgical rites litanies of various sorts, such as intercessions and supplications (the Litany of the Saints), by their nature should be sung (see STL 115c). The singing of these various litanies during the various liturgical rites will be addressed throughout Part III of this book.

Finally, hymns, although not typically sung during the Eucharist, are also part of some of the liturgical rites and obviously should be sung. The *Liber hymnarius* is a fine and recommended source for locating liturgical hymns.[3] Often times the rubric in the missal introducing a hymn suggests a suitable liturgical song as an

---

1. The singing of these two elements is addressed more completely in Chapter 6.

2. The singing of the psalms during the various liturgical rites is addressed throughout Part III of this book.

3. *Liber hymnarius* is the Gregorian Chant hymnal with updated texts set in a new version of the traditional notation developed by the monks of Solesmes. See *Liber Hymnarius* (Orleans, MA: Paraclete Press, 1983).

alternative. This description in the missal, "a suitable liturgical song," requires some clarification and guidelines so that the song alternatives carry the same meaning and be of the same nature as the given text. The text of the song should be doctrinally sound and the accompaniment suited to the part of the liturgical celebration (see STL 115d).[4]

Preparing the Parts to be Sung

The pastor, informed about the Church's norms for singing the Sacred Liturgy and conscious of his own duty in this regard, should moderate the preparations for the sung liturgical celebrations. The pastor rightfully is assisted in this task with the help of deacons and liturgical music ministers. Every parochial situation and circumstance will vary, but the leadership of the pastor and the assistance of skilled and competent liturgical musicians is essential to planning the parts to be sung. Often times a committee is engaged to assist in this important pastoral work. Such a committee will benefit from a careful reading of *Sing to the Lord* and other pertinent documents on the Sacred Liturgy and liturgical music.

Hearing the Sounds of the Liturgical Year

The first notes of the Exultet after the Light of Christ passes through the liturgical assembly on the Easter Vigil ring the sound of Easter in our believing ears, the sound of the Resurrection of our Lord from the dead. We look forward to this thrilling sound every year and know that it belongs to no other time. The sound of the Exultet with its text proclaims, "This is the night!"—"This is the night when Christ broke the prison bars of death, and rose victorious from the underworld."[5] The given chants for Palm Sunday of the Lord's Passion and the Sacred Easter Triduum should be a part of every parish repertoire with yearly efforts to teach them, sing them and pray them. The 1988 *Circular Letter, Paschale Solemnitatis: On Preparing*

---

4. The singing of a suitable liturgical song during the various liturgical rites is addressed throughout Part III of this book.

5. RM, Paschal Proclamation.

and Celebrating the Easter Feasts, speaks forcefully to this point.[6]
In planning the parts to be sung on Palm Sunday and during the Easter
Triduum, we should anticipate the use of these chants both with
the liturgical music ministries and with the faithful in mind as how
to best accomplish singing them.

The Bishops also remind us that another sound of the liturgical seasons is the silence or restraint of the organ or other musical
instruments (see STL 114). The introduction to the Season of Lent
in the new *Roman Missal* (2002) reminds us of what is already established in the *General Instruction of the Roman Missal*. "During
this season . . . the use of musical instruments is permitted
only to support singing. Nevertheless, Laetare Sunday (the Fourth
Sunday of Lent), Solemnities and Feasts are exceptions to this
rule."[7] "In Advent, the organ and other musical instruments should be
used with a moderation that is consistent with the season's character
and does not anticipate the full joy of the Nativity of the Lord."[8]

Selecting the Music for the Parts to be Sung

In *Sing to the Lord*, the Bishops consistently state that the primary role
of music in the celebration of the Liturgy is to help the members of
the gathered assembly join themselves to the action of Christ and to
give voice to the gift of faith (see STL 125). To ensure this primary
role and to make choices in keeping with what the liturgical rites
prescribe and mean, *Sing to the Lord*, similar to its antecedent *Music
in Catholic Worship*, identifies three judgments to guide the selection
of music to be sung. (see MCW 26–41) The three judgments are
liturgical, pastoral, and musical. These three judgments ultimately
reduce to one evaluation: Is this selection of music—given all the
parameters, options, and requirements of the Sacred Liturgy—the
most appropriate choice?

All three judgments must be considered together, and no
individual judgment can be applied in isolation from the other two.
This evaluation requires cooperation, consultation, collaboration, and

---

6. See (PS) 32 and 42.

7. RM, Introduction to the Season of Lent, 4; See also GIRM 313.

8. GIRM 313.

mutual respect among those who are skilled in any of the three judgments, be they pastors, musicians, liturgists, or planners.[9]

Before any evaluation and judgment can be made on the quality of liturgical music, several other factors need to be in place. The pastor, and also the priest celebrant of the rites, is responsible in an overall way for the liturgical music sung during the celebration of the Sacred Liturgy. Pastors and priest celebrants of the Sacred Liturgy, mindful they are servants of the Mystery they celebrate, need to place the spiritual and liturgical needs of the assembly before their own when planning what music to use (see STL 119, GIRM, 352). When the pastor or priest celebrant includes the collaborative efforts of liturgical music ministers and other representative members of the liturgical assembly, the preparation of liturgical music will be more comprehensive, using more of the available liturgical options and seamlessly executing the actual celebration (see STL 120–121).

How to Judge the Qualities of Liturgical Music

Sing to the Lord offers several important aspects of the care that should govern the choice for liturgical music as a preface to its evaluation and judgment. The U.S. Bishops offer this wise counsel, "Effective preparation of liturgical song that fosters the maximum participation of the gathered assembly is a cooperative venture that respects the essential role of a variety of persons with mutual competencies."[10] Every celebration of the Sacred Liturgy includes dimension beyond liturgical music which additionally need to be considered:
- the spoken elements of the celebration;
- the type of liturgical celebration;
- the nature of the liturgical assembly;
- various aspects of the liturgical environment; and
- the unique features of the rite itself to be celebrated (see STL 123).

All of these considerations need to be combined with the oversight of the pastor and duties of the liturgical music ministers in order to

9. STL 126.
10. STL 122.

begin to evaluate and judge the quality of the proposed liturgical music, keeping in mind its musical and textual features (see STL 124).

What follows now is the complete description of the liturgical, pastoral, and musical judgment in *Sing to the Lord*.

The Liturgical Judgment

The question asked by this judgment may be stated as follows: Is this composition capable of meeting the structural and textual requirements set forth by the liturgical books for this particular rite?

Structural considerations depend on the demands of the rite itself to guide the choice of parts to be sung, taking into account the principle of progressive solemnity. A certain balance among the various elements of the liturgy should be sought, so that less important elements do not overshadow more important ones. Textual elements include the ability of a musical setting to support the liturgical text and to convey meaning faithful to the teaching of the Church.

A brief introduction to the aspects of music and the various liturgical rites is provided in nos. 137ff of STL. (See Chapters 6 through 9 of this book.) Pastoral musicians should develop a working familiarity with the requirements of each rite through a study of the liturgical books themselves. (STL 127–129)

The liturgical judgment focuses on the rite itself. This important consideration is the starting point for beginning to evaluate and judge the quality of liturgical music coming from what is suggested in the liturgical books themselves. We need to be convinced of the value of this starting point as the first way that singing the Sacred Liturgy is indeed worship of God. So, the liturgical choice highlights the rite—its structure and text—and asks if the liturgical music adequately communicates the meaning of both.

The Pastoral Judgment

The pastoral judgment considers the actual community gathered to celebrate in a particular place at a particular time. Does a musical composition promote the sanctification of the members of the liturgical assembly by drawing them closer to the holy mysteries being celebrated? Does it strengthen their formation in faith by opening their hearts to the mystery being celebrated on this occasion or in this season? Is it capable of expressing the faith that God has planted in their hearts and summoned them to celebrate?

In the dioceses of the United States of America today, liturgical assemblies are composed of people of many different nations. Such peoples often "have their own musical tradition, and this plays a great part in their religious and social life. For this reason their music should be held in proper esteem and a suitable place is to be given to it, not only in forming their religious sense but also in adapting worship to their native genius."[11]

Other factors—such as the age, culture, language, and education of a given liturgical assembly—must also be considered. Particular musical forms and the choice of individual compositions for congregational participation will often depend on those ways in which a particular group finds it easiest to join their hearts and minds to the liturgical action. Similarly, the musical experience of a given liturgical assembly is to be carefully considered, lest forms of musical expression that are alien to their way of worshiping be introduced precipitously. On the other hand, one should never underestimate the ability of persons of all ages, cultures, languages, and levels of education to learn something new and to understand things that are properly and thoroughly introduced.

The pastoral question, finally, is always the same: Will this composition draw this particular people closer to the mystery of Christ, which is at the heart of this liturgical celebration? (STL 130–133)

The pastoral judgment focuses on the liturgical assembly. The liturgical assembly can be described in many different ways, such as, the age, the culture, the language, and the faith experience of those gathered to celebrate the Sacred Liturgy. The overarching consideration underscoring the pastoral judgment is the assistance that the chosen liturgical music will give to the liturgical assembly to enter into the Mysteries of Christ and participate in these Mysteries both interiorly and exteriorly. The success of this participation includes an awareness of the liturgical and musical competencies of the liturgical assembly.

The Musical Judgment

The musical judgment asks whether this composition has the necessary aesthetic qualities that can bear the weight of the mysteries celebrated in the Liturgy. It asks the question: Is this composition technically, aesthetically, and expressively worthy?

11. SC 119. (Footnote from STL)

This judgment requires musical competence. Only artistically sound music will be effective and endure over time. To admit to the Liturgy the cheap, the trite, or the musical cliché often found in secular popular songs is to cheapen the Liturgy, to expose it to ridicule, and to invite failure.

Sufficiency of artistic expression, however, is not the same as musical style, for "the Church has not adopted any particular style of art as her own. She has admitted styles from every period, in keeping with the natural characteristics and conditions of peoples and the needs of the various rites."[12] Thus, in recent times, the Church has consistently recognized and freely welcomed the use of various styles of music as an aid to liturgical worship. (STL 134–136)

The musical judgment focuses on the music itself. The music must be good music, nothing trite or trendy, but of an enduring quality. This feature of the music is coextensive with an evaluation of its beauty and truth, of its aesthetic and expressive dimensions to communicate and manifest the very Mystery of Christ celebrated in the Sacred Liturgy. Perhaps this judgment seems very subjective. However, its objectivity is maintained when it is made in conjunction with the liturgical and pastoral judgments.

When we reach the point of making the liturgical, pastoral, and musical judgments, we must keep in mind the injunction in *Sing to the Lord* that all three ultimately become one judgment. What is the most appropriate choice to assist the liturgical assembly to join with the action of Christ and give voice to their gift of faith?

Again, here are the summary questions we need to ask in order to judge the quality of liturgical music:

- Is it appropriate?
- Is this composition capable of meeting the structural and textual requirements set forth by the liturgical books for this particular rite?
- Will this composition draw this particular people closer to the mystery of Christ, which is at the heart of this liturgical celebration?
- Is this composition technically, aesthetically, and expressively worthy?

With all that has already been said about singing the Sacred Liturgy and with these judgments in mind, the pastor and the liturgical music ministers can competently prepare for sung liturgical celebrations.

---

12. SC 123 (Footnote from STL)

CONCLUSION

Every dimension of the Church's liturgical rites teach us something about what we believe, even the way to prepare singing the liturgy. With its consideration of the parts of the liturgical rites, this chapter lays the groundwork for the discussions in Part III of this book on singing the Liturgy itself.

The celebration of the sacred Mysteries on a Sunday differs from celebration on a weekday. A processional chant differs obviously from singing a biblical response to the proclamation of the Word of God. In addition to calendar differences, the various parts and elements of the liturgical rites differ according to their specific nature and purpose. Part II of this book followed *Sing to the Lord* with an emphasis on the practice of the principle of progressive solemnity for planning what to sing. In Part III we will continue the application of the principle of progressive solemnity according to the parts of the liturgical rites to be sung. We will be careful and consistent when refering to the judgment tools to sing what is directed and described in the liturgical books.

Part III

Singing the Eucharist, the Other Sacraments, and Other Liturgical Rites

Singing the actual liturgy continues to be the pastoral practice of the Church. This practice arises from our liturgical tradition and is proposed consistently in the reformed liturgical books and magisterial documents on the subject. In Part III, we will carefully review what is established and suggested in the liturgical books for singing the liturgy today.

We will follow in most cases the outline given in *Sing to the Lord* for its presentation of liturgical music in the various liturgical rites. We will also discuss some of the liturgical books and rites not mentioned in *Sing to the Lord*. In this Part, we will examine all of the liturgical rites with an explicit focus and identification on what is said about singing the celebration. We recognize the importance and the need for more complete information and explanation, theologically and liturgically, to underscore what is sung and why it is sung in liturgical celebrations. To that end, in this part, we have included discussions (Notes and Comments) based on the introductions and the various liturgical books themselves.

The practice of actually singing the very texts found in the liturgical books and not substituting alternatives or imposing popular songs (although at times necessary and permitted), receives all of the Sacred Liturgy as it is given to us. This concept of the "given-ness" and, in this case, the use of the liturgical musical texts provided, restores the

Sacred Liturgy to its original theological place of forming the Christian people in the celebrated faith of the Church.

The celebration of the Eucharist, and indeed of all the rites, then can be trusted, that is when the given texts are sung, as a manifestation of the common faith and preserved from manipulation into something foreign and opposed to the faith. When the liturgical books, as will be seen below, allow for the replacement of the same text with a suitable alternative, what is given inspires both in text and context what should be sung. The choice of the text and its accompaniment describe, teach, and form those who sing them. This is a significant pastoral point for us to keep in mind when planning any celebration of the Sacred Liturgy. Thus, this book, as a guide to theologically and liturgically using *Sing to the Lord*, gives first preference to what the rites call for to be sung and only secondarily promotes the use of a suitable alternative.

When the liturgical book suggests an "appropriate" or "suitable" liturgical song as an alternative to what is given in the text, we do not suggest such examples in this companion. However, we encourage you to make such a selection, if necessary, on what has already been described in Parts I and II of this book with regard to what is "appropriate" or "suitable." These selections should be subject to the judgments for their liturgical, pastoral, and musical qualities. It is not the purpose of *Sing to the Lord* nor of this companion to actually identify what is appropriate or suitable. In fact, this companion, taking its cue from *Sing to the Lord*, endorses the singing of the given liturgical texts over imported texts, however suitable.

Often times when the liturgical books, even the vernacular editions, provide specific examples of texts, psalms, and antiphons to be sung, only the Latin example or at least its title is given. We repeat the Latin example when there is no official English alternative in the English language typical editions.

Documentation cited from the pertinent liturgical books allows for an emphasis on many of the points raised by *Sing to the Lord*. Some notes and comments then follow in many instances as a help to the pastor and liturgical music minister to see this emphasis with respect to a theological and liturgical dimension of singing the celebration.

Chapter 6

How Do We Sing the Eucharist?

Introduction

Sing the Eucharist! If any directive can be sounded with regard
to liturgical music throughout the last century and into this one with
the publication of the 2002 *General Instruction of the Roman Missal*,
it is to sing the Eucharist! The U.S. Bishops' document *Sing to
the Lord* understates this charge to sing the Eucharist. Singing the
Eucharist, which means to sing precisely the very texts found in
the *Roman Missal* (Sacramentary) and the *Lectionary for Mass*, belongs
to both the most solemn celebrations of the Mass in the diocesan
Cathedral as well as in the parish church and more simple celebrations
of the Mass on college campuses and in nursing homes.

The *General Instruction of the Roman Missal* and the current
edition of the *Roman Missal (Sacramentary)*[1] are the chief sources for
what is given for singing the Eucharist. Now, let's look at some
general ideas and then review the rites of the Mass.

Singing the Mass

What the General Instruction of the Roman Missal *Says*

Great importance should therefore be attached to the use of singing in
the celebration of the Mass, with due consideration for the culture of the
people and abilities of each liturgical assembly. Although it is not always

---

1. Hereafter in this Chapter the *Roman Missal* will only be listed as such and not as *Roman
Missal (Sacramentary)*, when speaking of the book in general. *Sacramentary* will be used when
referring to the current English translation of the *Missale Romanum*.

necessary (e.g., in weekday Masses) to sing all the texts that are of themselves meant to be sung, every care should be taken that singing by the
ministers and the people is not absent in celebrations that occur on Sundays
and on holy days of obligation.

In choosing the parts actually to be sung, however, preference should be
given to those that are of greater importance and especially to those to be
sung by the priest or the deacon or the lector, with the people responding,
or by the priest and people together. (GIRM 40)

Notes and Comments.   Number 40 of the *General Instruction of the
Roman Missal* densely includes several significant features of the
Church's practice of singing the Eucharist. First and above all, "great
importance should . . . be attached to the use of singing in the
celebration of Mass." This is the case even with "due consideration"
for the varied constituency of the liturgical assembly. Degrees of sung
celebrations from Sundays to weekdays are recognized. A "preference"
for singing belongs to the more important parts of the Eucharist
as well as to those parts which include a dialogue and the priest and
people singing together. These liturgical musical features of singing
the Eucharist summarize the same points in the 1967 *Musicam
Sacram*, the guiding liturgical music document in the course of the
reform of the liturgical books, especially the *Roman Missal.*[2]

Before continuing with a review of what should be sung in
the celebration of the Eucharist several other introductory and helpful
ideas need to be addressed.

What Is the Sung Ordinary of the Mass?

Some may consider this phrase, ordinary of the mass, dated or no
longer in use with the reformed *Roman Missal.* In fact, there is still an
Ordinary for the celebration of the Eucharist and knowing it assists
with the preparation of liturgical music. The Ordinary of the Mass
includes the *Kyrie,* the *Gloria,* the *Sanctus,* and the *Agnus Dei.* These
integrally musically composed fixed parts of the Sunday Mass tell us
by their very nature that the texts themselves should be sung and that
singing them gives solemn expression to the mystery celebrated.

---

2. The reader may want to review what *Musicam Sacram* describes about the preferences for
singing some parts of the Mass over others, as well as the application of GIRM 40 in Chapter 4
of this book.

The rules with regard to singing the Ordinary of the Mass have changed and are not as precise as in the past. According to the *General Instruction of the Roman Missal* the intent would be that, when the Ordinary could and should be sung, this would include all of its elements. However, as will be seen below, each of these parts can be carried out in different ways that might suggest one of the elements from one or another composition or the singing of some and not all. The present norms allow for flexibility depending on both the occasion and capacity of the liturgical assembly to sing.

Prior to the reform, the sung Latin Ordinary of the Mass had a variety of compositions and some of these came to be associated with the liturgical seasons and specific liturgical observances such as those of the Blessed Virgin Mary, the Apostles, and the Mass for the Dead. In this way, the sound of the Ordinary indicated to those singing and listening the time of the year and the commemoration. This association, one more of tradition than law, provided another example of the liturgical music itself augmenting the text with a context. The same possibility exists when singing the Ordinary of the Mass in English or Spanish or in any of the vernacular languages. The choice of the composition might not only include fidelity to the approved translation but also a composition whose sound lends itself or can become associated with a particular liturgical season or liturgical observance.

Although the U.S. Bishops do not address this in *Sing to the Lord*, frequently American liturgical musical composers include, along with the Ordinary of the Mass, a setting for the anamnesis and the "Amen" of the Eucharistic Prayer. Both of these parts of the Eucharistic Prayer are dialogues between the priest celebrant and the people. The priest acclaims the Mystery of Faith and the people respond in one of several ways. The priest sings the doxology and the people assent, "Amen." These two dialogues, although of a quite significant importance especially in the context of the Eucharistic Prayer, are like all the dialogues of the Eucharist. They are a liturgical exchange between the priest and the people. They are not rites or parts that stand alone like the *Sanctus*. Thus, their musical form, a form provided in the *Roman Missal*, as with all of the other dialogues, should be in accord with the nature of the anamnesis and this "Amen." They are, after all, dialogues!

What Is the Sung Proper of the Mass?

The sung Proper of the Mass includes those texts assigned to a liturgical season or liturgical observance. The Propers include the Entrance and Communion chants of the Mass among other parts. Presently, these texts and their chants are not available in an approved vernacular translation. The Latin source, which also includes the Offertory chant, is the *Graduale Romanum*, which the *General Instruction of the Roman Missal* does list as the first option for the Entrance, Offertory, and Communion (GIRM 48, 74, 87). An additional Latin source that provides a series of common selections for these same parts of the Mass for the liturgical seasons and some liturgical observances is the *Graduale Simplex*, which the *General Instruction* lists as well (GIRM 48, 74, 87). The Responsorial Psalm and the verse before the Gospel from the *Lectionary for Mass* might also be considered as part of the Proper of the Mass. The proper Latin Gradual and Tract, options for the Responsorial Psalm as indicated in the *General Instruction*, can also be found in the *Graduale Romanum*.

We need to encourage new vernacular musical compositions of these Latin liturgical texts to foster the singing of the Proper of the Mass in our liturgical assemblies. In the meantime, it is possible to make use of related English liturgical musical texts to begin to once again sing the Proper of the Mass.

What is a Solemn Celebration of the Eucharist on Sunday?

The *General Instruction of the Roman Missal* recognizes degrees of solemnity in the celebration of the Mass with the more solemn celebrations occurring on Sundays and solemnities.[3] These degrees of solemnity apply equally to music as to ceremony, vesture, and the general comportment of all aspects of the celebration. We addressed the guiding liturgical musical principle for progressive solemnity in the Sacred Liturgy in Chapter 4. The question at hand with regard to a solemn celebration of the Eucharist concerns itself both with an application of this principle as well as the practice of a more solemn form of the sung Eucharist in the parish each Sunday and solemnity.

Keep in mind that such a sung Eucharist, that is, singing all of the texts intended to be sung and with the priest and people

---

3. See again GIRM 40.

assisted by a choir or at least sufficient musical leadership, has as one
of its purposes a full expression of the faith celebrated in the Mysteries
for the glory of the Lord and the ever deepening holiness of the
liturgical assembly. Singing the Eucharist is not superficial in any way!
Often, solemn celebrations of the Eucharist mark special occasions
and events in the life of a parish or a member of the Church and
they should do so. However, and more to the point, these same sung
solemn celebrations should take place in a typical way from Sunday
to Sunday with the resources available to communicate, manifest, and
celebrate the faith. This is fundamentally why we sing the Eucharist
and why it should be sung solemnly on Sundays.

A solemn celebration of the Eucharist in the parish on
Sundays and solemnities, first of all, requires the necessary musical
resources, such as instruments, a choir or schola, a psalmist, and
possibly a leader of the singing for the liturgical assembly. The priest,
deacon, and the people should be expected to sing consistently the
dialogues throughout the course of the Eucharist. The ordinary and
proper texts, or their suitable liturgical alternatives, should be sung.
The solemn celebration of the Eucharist could be, for example, the
parish occasion for the celebration of the rites of Christian Initiation,
the Baptism of Children, and Marriage.

What is the Musical Notation in the Roman Missal?

The *Roman Missal* itself provides the musical notation for those parts
of the missal that are sung between the priest and the people and
for the Eucharistic Prayer. In fact, the 2002 edition of the *Missale
Romanum* includes as part of the Order of Mass these musical
notations for all of the dialogues beginning with the sign of the cross
and greeting during the Introductory Rites. The rules for translation
found in the 2001 *Liturgiam authenticam* mandate that the vernacular liturgical book should imitate the Latin typical edition in
its structure and content.[4] These same musical notations will be in
the anticipated English language Roman Missal. The point here
is twofold.

First, the texts intended to be sung in the course of the
Eucharist by the priest and people in dialogue and the most important

---

4. See LA 109–125.

prayer text of the Eucharist, the Eucharistic Prayer, are highlighted as typically sung texts by the liturgical book itself. Singing these texts is the norm. Not singing these texts is not the norm even for less solemn occasions.

Second, the musical notations given in the *Roman Missal* form part of the auditory translation of the texts, part of the sung sound of these texts, and thus part of their meaning for the singer and listener. This sung sound is a constitutive element of the Roman Rite as part of the way the Church prays in addition to the words. These musical notations should not be set aside too easily unless the priest celebrant cannot sing them in a suitable and dignified manner.

A priest who cannot sing the texts should be mindful that his spoken proclamation of the same texts, or at least a singing of some of them *in recto tono* (on one pitch), should highlight their significance in the course of the celebration of the Eucharist.

Sing to the Lord consistently omits a reference to the musical notation both in the Latin and English editions of the *Roman Missal,* for the sung parts of the priest and people in the Order of Mass, including the Collect and other presidential prayers. These musical notations are highlighted below to encourage the singing of these parts of the Mass in the tradition of the Roman Rite.

What are the Titles for the Parts of the Mass?

The titles used in this book for the parts of the Mass are those used in the 2002 English translation of the *General Instruction of the Roman Missal.* A consistent and faithful use of these titles assists with an understanding of the various parts of the Mass and avoids titles and names that do not clearly describe these same parts.

These introductory concepts, which we have discussed with regard to the Ordinary and Proper of the Mass, solemn celebrations of the Eucharist, attentiveness to the musical notation in the *Roman Missal,* and to the titles of the parts of the Mass, form an interactive backdrop for singing the Eucharist as we now review each of the parts and elements of the Mass. Preparing the sung Mass, rightfully stated by the U.S. Bishops in *Sing to the Lord,* requires knowledge of the parts and elements of the celebration, the nature and relationship of these parts and elements, and "the overall rhythm of the liturgical action" (see STL 137).

Introductory Rites

Entrance Chant

What the General Instruction of the Roman Missal *Says*

> After the people have gathered, the Entrance chant begins as the priest enters with the deacon and ministers. The purpose of this chant is to open the celebration, foster the unity of those who have been gathered, introduce their thoughts to the mystery of the liturgical season or festivity, and accompany the procession of the priest and ministers. (GIRM 47)
>
> The singing at this time is done either alternately by the choir and the people or in a similar way by the cantor and the people, or entirely by the people, or by the choir alone. In the dioceses of the United States of America there are four options for the Entrance Chant: (1) the antiphon from the Roman Missal or the Psalm from the Roman Gradual as set to music there or in another musical setting; (2) the seasonal antiphon and Psalm of the Simple Gradual; (3) a song from another collection of psalms and antiphons, approved by the Conference of Bishops or the diocesan Bishop, including psalms arranged in responsorial or metrical forms; (4) a suitable liturgical song similarly approved by the Conference of Bishops or the diocesan Bishop.
>
> If there is no singing at the entrance, the antiphon in the Missal is recited either by the faithful, or by some of them, or by a lector; otherwise, it is recited by the priest himself, who may even adapt it as an introductory explanation (cf. n. 31). (GIRM 48)

Notes and Comments. Entrance chant is the appropriate title for this part of the Introductory Rites since the priest and faithful are already gathered by Christ and now *enter* into the celebration of his Sacred Mysteries. We explain here in greater detail the use of the options for the Entrance chant which are only listed in *Sing to the Lord* (see STL 144). This chant actually begins the celebration of the Mass and concurs with the whole of the procession of the sacred ministers until the priest celebrant takes his place at the chair. This would also include, if opportune, the incensation of the altar. The preference is to sing the word of the Lord from the psalms. In making the choice

for a psalm or a suitable liturgical song other than the proper, attention should be given to the selection of the text so that the sense
of the given text is not arbitrarily set aside. When choosing to sing a
suitable liturgical song over the given proper or appropriate psalm and
antiphon, this choice should be guided by the three judgments for
liturgical music described above. A doxology is not required in the use
of a psalm; however, with songs it is important to be inclusive of the
three Divine Persons either in the whole of the hymn or its
doxological conclusion (see STL 143).

To date, the Conference of Bishops has not approved any
particular collection of psalms and antiphons nor have the Bishops
approved a collection of liturgical songs (see STL 144b). So, the
liturgical music planner should consult the choices given in the
Graduale Romanum or the given antiphon for recitation as sources
to inspire the Entrance chant when looking for other options.
Again, while a preference is for the faithful to sing the Entrance
chant, it can be carried out in other ways as noted above in the
General Instruction of the Roman Missal.[5]

The listing of the four options above for the Entrance chant
belongs to the series of adaptations by the Bishops of the United
States to the *General Instruction of the Roman Missal.* It is important
to note at this point that option one for the Entrance chant has
been amended as of November 2007 by the US Bishops so that the
antiphon provided in the *Roman Missal* is no longer among the sung
possibilities for the Entrance chant. The antiphon in the *Roman
Missal* was never intended to be sung but rather to be recited when no
singing occurred. This amendment also applies to what is currently
in the General Instruction for the Offertory and Communion chant.
Confirmation of this amendment awaits a recognition of the Holy See.

Act of Penitence

The *Roman Missal* provides three forms for the Act of Penitence.
All three forms include an introduction which may be sung by the

5. An interesting resource to consider is Christoph Tietze, *Hymn Introits for the Liturgical Year: The Origin and Early Development of the Latin Texts* (Chicago: Hillenbrand Books, 2005). The author has composed congregational settings of the proper parts of the Mass for the liturgical year. The accompaniment book, *Introit Hymns for the Church Year,* is available from World Library Publications.

priest celebrant. The absolution, which is the same in all three forms, may also be sung by the priest celebrant with the faithful responding "Amen." In the first form all recite the "I confess" together. In the second form, the versicles and responses may be sung by the priest celebrant. In the third form, the invocations, always addressed to the Lord, may be sung by the deacon or cantor or, in their absence, by the priest celebrant. Invocations other than those in the *Roman Missal* can be written for the third form inspired by the biblical texts or the liturgical season or observance (see STL 145). In the *Sacramentary*, the tones for the second and third forms of the Act of Penitence are found in Appendix III: The Order of Mass.

Kyrie

What the General Instruction of the Roman Missal *Says*

> After the Act of Penitence, the Kyrie is always begun, unless it has already been included as part of the Act of Penitence. Since it is a chant by which the faithful acclaim the Lord and implore his mercy, it is ordinarily done by all, that is, by the people and the choir or cantor having a part in it.
>
> As a rule, each acclamation is sung or said twice, though it may be repeated several times, by reason of the character of the various languages, as well as of the artistry of the music, or of other circumstances. When the Kyrie is sung as a part of the Act of Penitence, a trope may precede each acclamation. (GIRM 52)

Notes and Comments.   The *Kyrie* is always used with the first and second form of the Act of Penitence. Consideration should be given to singing this in Greek which is consistent with its original form. *Sing to the Lord* limits the sung form of this litany (see STL 146). Actually, there are many ways to sing the *Kyrie*, ranging from a very simple form to a more complex ornate form. The choice should include its relationship to the other parts of the sung ordinary and the liturgical season and observance as well as the manner in which it will be sung, that is, by all or in alternation.

Blessing and Sprinkling of Holy Water

What the General Instruction of the Roman Missal *Says*

On Sundays, especially in the Season of Easter, in place of the customary Act of Penitence, from time to time the blessing and sprinkling of water to recall Baptism may take place. (GIRM 51)

Notes and Comments. The priest celebrant may sing the introduction, the blessing of the water, and the conclusion after sprinkling the faithful. Song always accompanies the sprinkling of the faithful. The following information supplements *Sing to the Lord* as a help to pastors and liturgical music ministers for the song that accompanies this rite. The choice for this song could include what is given in the tradition or inspired by the tradition. The *Roman Missal* provides several options. Outside of paschal time, the antiphons include: *Asperges me* (Psalms 51:9); *Effundam super* (Ezra 36:25–26) with a psalm; or the hymn *Benedictus Deus* (cf. 1 Peter 1:3–5). In paschal time, the antiphons include: *Vidi aquam* (Ezra 47:1–2, 9); *In die resurrectionis meae* (cf. Wisdom 3:8; Ezra 36:5); *Fontes et omnia* (cf. Daniel 3:77, 79); *Vos genus electum* (1 Peter 2:9); *E latere tuo* (see *Missale Romanum*). When *Sing to the Lord* directs that "[t]he song accompanying the sprinkling with blessed water should have an explicitly baptismal character," it restricts the variety of options provided by the tradition for this song (see STL 147). This song may be sung by all or in alternation depending on the choice made.

Gloria

What the General Instruction of the Roman Missal *Says*

The Gloria is a very ancient and venerable hymn in which the Church, gathered together in the Holy Spirit, glorifies and entreats God the Father and the Lamb. The text of this hymn may not be replaced by any other text. The Gloria is intoned by the priest or, if appropriate, by a cantor or by the choir, but it is sung either by everyone together, or by the people alternately with the choir, or by the choir alone. If not sung, it is to be recited either by all together or by two parts of the congregation responding one to the other.

It is sung or said on Sundays outside the Seasons of Advent and Lent, on solemnities and feasts, and at special celebrations of a more solemn character. (GIRM 53)

Notes and Comments.   The *Gloria* should be sung especially during the seasons of Christmas and Easter and, if possible, whenever it is prescribed on a Sunday or solemnity. The *Gloria* constitutes an independent rite and therefore its place and use cannot be rearranged (see GIRM 37). For example, the Gloria should not serve as a choice for the Entrance chant or accompany the sprinkling with holy water (see STL 150). Again, no substitutions can be made for the *Gloria* (see STL 148; see also GIRM 53, 366). In keeping with the Roman liturgical tradition, as indicated by the *General Instruction of the Roman Missal,* a preference should be given to the priest celebrant intoning the *Gloria* (see STL 149).

The Bishops' Committee on the Liturgy *Policy for the Approval of Musical Compositions for the Liturgy, Number 2.* is quoted in *Sing to the Lord* which allows for the use of refrains in the singing of the *Gloria* (see STL 149).[6] The structure of this hymn as a single text in three parts, as well as the Roman musical tradition with regard to the *Gloria,* challenges the appropriateness of the use of a refrain. The *Gloria,* however, can be sung in a great variety of ways, especially in alternation, which encourages participation by all (see STL 149).

Collect

What the General Instruction of the Roman Missal *Says*

The Collect with its introduction and the "Amen" of the faithful should be sung on Sundays and solemnities. Sample tones for the Collect are found in the *Missale Romanum,* Appendix I: *Cantus varii in ordine Missae occurrentes,* and the *Sacramentary,* Appendix III: The Order of Mass.

The Bishops suggest in *Sing to the Lord* that "[e]ven when the Collect is not sung, the conclusion to the prayer may be sung, along with the response by the people" (STL 151). While this sugges-tion encourages sung prayer, it neglects to account for the integrity of the whole of the Collect when it separates out some its parts for song

---

6. See *Policy For the Approval of Musical Compsitions for the Liturgy,* Number 2.

over other parts. It must be recalled that one of the chief reasons for singing the liturgy is to give solemn expression to the faith of the Church communicated in its many parts. The body of the Collect is where this faith is expressed and so it should be sung as well.

LITURGY OF THE WORD

The Readings and the Gospel

Notes and Comments.   Typically the readings appointed for the Liturgy of the Word are read in an appropriate voice.[7] The *Lectionary for Mass* indicates that for more solemn occasions these same readings may be chanted according to English tones inspired by the *Ordo Cantus Missae* (see STL 153).[8] Above all, on more solemn occasions the Gospel may be chanted when the other readings are read (see STL 168).[9] *Sing to the Lord* overlooks the occasions when the biblical texts themselves could be sung; however, it is important to note that the tonal choice is not arbitrary but is guided and inspired by what is provided in the typical Latin edition.

In any case, even when the readings are not sung, the solemnity of the occasion may suggest the acclamations at the conclusion of each reading and the response of the faithful may be sung as well as the introduction to the Gospel (see STL 154, 169).[10]

Responsorial Psalm

What the General Instruction of the Roman Missal *Says*

After the first reading comes the responsorial Psalm, which is an integral part of the Liturgy of the Word and holds great liturgical and pastoral importance, because it fosters meditation on the word of God.

The responsorial Psalm should correspond to each reading and should, as a rule, be taken from the *Lectionary for Mass*.

---

7. See LFM 14.

8. See LFM 14.

9. See LFM 14.

10. See LFM 17, 18. While it is possible for the cantor to sing the acclamation that concludes the readings, lectors should be trained to carry out this role as part of their ministry.

It is preferable that the responsorial Psalm be sung, at least as far as the people's response is concerned. Hence, the psalmist, or the cantor of the Psalm, sings the verses of the Psalm from the ambo or another suitable place. The entire congregation remains seated and listens, but, as a rule, takes part by singing the response, except when the Psalm is sung straight through without a response. In order, however, that the people may be able to sing the Psalm response more readily, texts of some responses and Psalms have been chosen for the various seasons of the year or for the various categories of saints. These may be used in place of the text corresponding to the reading whenever the Psalm is sung. If the Psalm cannot be sung, then it should be recited in such a way that it is particularly suited to fostering meditation on the word of God.

In the dioceses of the United States of America, the following may also be sung in place of the Psalm assigned in the Lectionary for Mass: either the proper or seasonal antiphon and Psalm from the Lectionary, as found either in the Roman Gradual or Simple Gradual, or, in another musical setting; or, an antiphon and Psalm from another collection of the psalms and antiphons, including psalms arranged in metrical form, providing that they have been approved by the United States Conference of Catholic Bishops or the diocesan Bishop. Songs or hymns may not be used in place of the responsorial Psalm. (GIRM 61)

Notes and Comments. The Responsorial Psalm is the word of God. As the *General Instruction of the Roman Missal* provides for many sources for the Responsorial Psalm, above all the *Lectionary for Mass*, it does so with the provision that alternatives to the one given in the *Lectionary* will also be the word of God. One of these alternatives includes a metrical form for the Responsorial Psalm. The bishops remind us in *Sing to the Lord* of this same allowance (see STL 158). *However, a caution needs to be raised here. A metrical form of the psalm must be the text of the psalm and not a loosely paraphrased song or hymn based on a psalm (see STL 159).*

The Responsorial Psalm announces the Word of God although the manner of proclamation differs from other parts of the Liturgy of the Word. Preference should be given to the singing of the Responsorial Psalm in every Mass (see STL 156). Typically, the appointed psalm is sung (see STL 157). If the verses of the psalm cannot be sung then at least the refrain could by sung by the faithful (see STL 160). The above norms from the *General Instruction* provided for the singing of the psalm encourages its sung form with differing ways of singing it (see STL 156).

Consideration should be given to the use of the many options for the Responsorial Psalm in the *Lectionary for Mass* and described in the *General Instruction of the Roman Missal* for the sake of singing the psalm. The use of the common psalm for the different seasons is a way to encourage the sung responsorial psalm (see STL 157). Consideration should also be ascribed to the liturgical tradition as found in the *Graduale Romanum* or the *Graduale Simplex* (see STL 158). To date, there are no other collections of psalms and antiphons approved by the Conference of Bishops for use as the Responsorial Psalm (see STL 158).

The Acclamation before the Gospel

What the General Instruction of the Roman Missal *Says*

After the reading that immediately precedes the Gospel, the Alleluia or another chant indicated by the rubrics is sung, as required by the liturgical season. An acclamation of this kind constitutes a rite or act in itself, by which the assembly of the faithful welcomes and greets the Lord who is about to speak to them in the Gospel, and professes its faith by means of the chant. It is sung by all while standing, and is led by the choir or a cantor, being repeated if this is appropriate. The verse, however, is sung either by the choir or by the cantor.

a. The Alleluia is sung in every season other than Lent. The verses are taken from the Lectionary or the Gradual.
b. During Lent, in place of the Alleluia, the verse before the Gospel is sung, as indicated in the Lectionary. It is also permissible to sing another psalm or tract, as found in the Gradual.

When there is only one reading before the Gospel:
a. During a season when the Alleluia is to be said, either the Alleluia Psalm or the responsorial Psalm followed by the Alleluia with its verse may be used.
b. During the season when the Alleluia is not to be said, either the psalm and the verse before the Gospel or the psalm alone may be used.
c. The Alleluia or verse before the Gospel may be omitted if they are not sung. (GIRM 62, 63)

Notes and Comments.   Typically the acclamation is sung before the Gospel as described above (see STL 161). During most of the Church Year, the Alleluia with the proper verse precedes the Gospel. During Lent any one of the eight chant texts provided in the *Lectionary for Mass* is used (see STL 163). The whole of the acclamation includes the Alleluia or chant and the verse. The proper verse, usually from the *Lectionary for Mass*, announces the Lord who will speak with his own word in the Gospel (see STL 161).

By way of further explanation beyond that in *Sing to the Lord* (see STL 164), the *General Instruction of the Roman Missal* and the *Introduction for the Lectionary for Mass* offer a variety of ways to carry out the acclamation before the Gospel, especially when there is only one reading before the Gospel as noted above.[11] The option of the Alleluia Psalm should be considered especially during the paschal time (see STL 164). Also, the options found in the *Graduale Romanum* could be carried out by the parish choir or schola.

The acclamation before the Gospel concurs with the whole of the ritual preparation for the proclamation of the Gospel (see GIRM 131–133, 175). So, the Alleluia or chant begins when all rise after the silence following the Second Reading or the Responsorial Psalm. This acclamation and verse, with the possible addition of other verses from the *Lectionary for Mass*, continues through the imposition of incense, if used, the blessing or prayer of the sacred minister and the procession with the *Book of the Gospels* to the ambo (see STL 161). After the proclamation of the Gospel, the Alleluia or chant—even the melody—is not repeated since its purpose is to welcome and greet the Lord who speaks his own Gospel. Instrumental music may follow the Gospel especially on those occasions when the *Book of the Gospels* is taken to the Bishop for veneration and the blessing of the people.

While it is permitted to recite or even omit the Alleluia or chant with the verse before the Gospel when not sung, every effort should be given to singing this rite which corresponds to its nature.

---

11. See also LFM 23.

Sequence

What the General Instruction of the Roman Missal *Says*

> The Sequence, which is optional except on Easter Sunday and on
> Pentecost Day, is sung before the Alleluia (GIRM 64).

Notes and Comments.   The *Lectionary for Mass* provides Sequences
on Easter Sunday and Pentecost Sunday at the Masses during the day
and for the Solemnity of the Body and Blood of the Lord and the
Memorial of Our Lady of Sorrows. The Sequences on Easter Sunday
and Pentecost Day are obligatory. A Sequence occurs before the
Acclamation before the Gospel (see STL 165).

Sequences are rare examples of hymns that occur during
the celebration of the Eucharist. Thus, they are typically sung.
The *General Instruction* provides little information as does the
Lectionary for Mass on how the Sequence is to be sung. Traditionally
the Sequence is sung in through-composed form. In *Sing to the
Lord* the Bishops suggest a variety of ways to sing the Sequence like
those proposed for the *Gloria* and the Creed, that is, by all or in
alternation (see STL 166). The current edition of the *Lectionary
for Mass* (1981/1998) offers only a poetic translation of the Sequences.
Sing to the Lord suggests that a metrical paraphrase of the Sequence
may be sung but does not provide a source for this provision except
that it be found in an approved collection of liturgical songs (see
STL 166). As of this writing there are no approved collection of liturgical songs which could serve as one of the Sequences.

The Profession of Faith or Creed

What the General Instruction of the Roman Missal *Says*

> The purpose of the Symbolum or Profession of Faith, or Creed, is that the
> whole gathered people may respond to the word of God proclaimed in the
> readings taken from Sacred Scripture and explained in the homily, and
> that they may also call to mind and confess the great mysteries of the faith
> by reciting the rule of faith in a formula approved for liturgical use, before
> these mysteries are celebrated in the Eucharist.

The Creed is to be sung or said by the priest together with the people on Sundays and solemnities. It may be said also at particular celebrations of a more solemn character.

If it is sung, it is begun by the priest or, if this is appropriate, by a cantor or by the choir. It is sung, however, either by all together or by the people alternating with the choir.

If not sung, it is to be recited by all together or by two parts of the assembly responding one to the other. (GIRM 67, 68)

Notes and Comments.   In the United States, the priest and faithful typically recite the Profession of Faith on Sundays and solemnities. However, for more solemn celebrations of the Eucharist, a sung Creed should be considered with a preference for the priest celebrant intoning it. The *General Instruction of the Roman Missal* offers a variety of ways to carry out the sung Creed, by all or in alternation, and also suggests that the Creed sung in Latin may be a valuable pastoral option (see GIRM 41). The Bishops in *Sing to the Lord* indicate that a congregational refrain may be helpful for the participation of the faithful in the sung Creed (see STL 170). However, this practice unnecessarily disrupts the form of the Profession of Faith as a single series of the articles of Faith.

Prayer of the Faithful

What the General Instruction of the Roman Missal *Says*

In the Prayer of the Faithful, the people respond in a certain way to the word of God which they have welcomed in faith and, exercising the office of their baptismal priesthood, offer prayers to God for the salvation of all. It is fitting that such a prayer be included, as a rule, in Masses celebrated with a congregation, so that petitions will be offered for the holy Church, for civil authorities, for those weighed down by various needs, for all men and women, and for the salvation of the whole world.

It is for the priest celebrant to direct this prayer from the chair. He himself begins it with a brief introduction, by which he invites the faithful to pray, and likewise he concludes it with a prayer. The intentions announced should be sober, succinct, composed freely but prudently, and should express the prayer of the entire community.

The intentions are announced from the ambo or from another suitable place, by the deacon or by a cantor, a lector, or by one of the lay faithful.

The people, however, stand and give expression to their prayer either by an invocation said together after each intention or by praying in silence. (GIRM 69, 71)

Notes and Comments.   The priest celebrant may sing the introduction to the Prayer of the Faithful, which is always addressed to the faithful and its conclusion with the short ending, "Through Christ our Lord." The intentions may also be sung either in their entirety or only the invitation to prayer and response to each intention. The Bishops add that even the response only might be sung (see STL 171).
It seems as with all other dialogues that the response in song should follow a sung invitation. Looking at the Prayer of the Faithful in its entirety suggests that all of its parts be sung in more solemn celebrations of the Eucharist.

The series of intentions are typically sung by the deacon at the ambo; however, in the absence of the deacon or, in favor of their being sung, the cantor may sing these same intentions at the ambo or another suitable place. The tone for the intentions should keep in mind the litanic form of the Prayer of the Faithful. The text of the invitations to prayer and the response should vary according to the liturgical season and observance. Although not mentioned in *Sing to the Lord*, the option for the faithful to respond with a corporate act of silence at times can take place with sung intentions. Sample ways of singing various invitations to prayer and responses can be found in the *Sacramentary:* Appendix III.

LITURGY OF THE EUCHARIST

Offertory Chant

What the General Instruction of the Roman Missal *Says*

The procession bringing the gifts is accompanied by the Offertory chant (cf. no. 37b), which continues at least until the gifts have been placed on the altar. The norms on the manner of singing are the same as for the Entrance chant (cf. no. 48). Singing may always accompany the rite at the offertory, even when there is no procession with the gifts (GIRM, 74).

The singing at this time is done either alternately by the choir and the people or in a similar way by the cantor and the people, or entirely by the people, or by the choir alone. In the dioceses of the United States of

America there are four options for the Entrance Chant: (1) the antiphon from the Roman Missal or the Psalm from the Roman Gradual as set to music there or in another musical setting; (2) the seasonal antiphon and Psalm of the Simple Gradual; (3) a song from another collection of psalms and antiphons, approved by the Conference of Bishops or the diocesan Bishop, including psalms arranged in responsorial or metrical forms; (4) a suitable liturgical song similarly approved by the Conference of Bishops or the diocesan Bishop. (GIRM 48)

Notes and Comments.   The Offertory chant, which begins after the conclusion of the Prayer of the Faithful, signals the beginning of the Liturgy of the Eucharist. This chant continues at least until the gifts are placed on the altar as indicated above and in *Sing to the Lord* (see STL 173). The preference is for this chant to accompany the procession of gifts and also while they are being set aside on the altar for the Sacrifice of the Lord. Thus, the chant corresponds to the whole action of the presentation of the gifts by the faithful and their presentation by the priest celebrant at the altar. Singing may always accompany the preparation of the altar and the gifts even when there is no procession with the gifts. When incense is used, the chant or at least its accompaniment should continue until the priest celebrant is ready to say, "Pray brethren."

Although the *General Instruction of the Roman Missal* provides a list of sources for the Offertory chant similar to those for the Entrance and Communion chants such availability is limited either in terms of approved translations or approved texts. Often times the choice is option four, a suitable liturgical song, which should be inspired by the liturgical season or observance, as well as this part of the Mass. Instrumental music suited for the celebration of the Sacred Liturgy may be an additional option outside of Lent (see STL 174).

Prayer over the Offerings

Notes and Comments.   The Prayer over the Offerings and the "Amen" of the faithful should be sung on Sundays and solemnities. Sample tones are found in the *Missale Romanum*: Appendix I: *Cantus varii in ordine Missae occurrentes,* and the *Sacramentary: The Order of Mass* and Alppendix III.

Sing to the Lord suggests that "[e]ven when the prayer is not sung, the conclusion to the prayer may be sung, along with the response by the people" (STL 175). This suggestion, as already treated above with the Collect, fails to account for the integrity of the whole of the prayer when it separates out some its parts for song over others.

The Eucharistic Prayer

What the General Instruction of the Roman Missal *Says*

The chief elements making up the Eucharistic Prayer may be distinguished in this way:

a. Thanksgiving (expressed especially in the Preface): in which the priest, in the name of the entire holy people, glorifies God the Father and gives thanks for the whole work of salvation or for some special aspect of it that corresponds to the day, festivity, or season.

b. Acclamation: in which the whole congregation, joining with the heavenly powers, sings the Sanctus. This acclamation, which is part of the Eucharistic Prayer itself, is sung or said by all the people with the priest.

c. Epiclesis: in which by means of particular invocations, the Church implores the power of the Holy Spirit that the gifts offered by human hands be consecrated, that is, become Christ's Body and Blood, and that the spotless Victim to be received in Communion be for the salvation of those who will partake of it.

d. Institution narrative and consecration: by means of words and actions of Christ, the Sacrifice is carried out which Christ himself instituted at the Last Supper, when he offered his Body and Blood under the species of bread and wine, and gave them to his Apostles to eat and drink, and left them the command to perpetuate this same mystery.

e. Anamnesis: in which the Church, fulfilling of the command that she received from Christ the Lord through the Apostles, keeps the memorial of Christ, recalling especially his blessed Passion, glorious Resurrection and Ascension into heaven.

f. Offering: by which, in this very memorial, the Church—and in particular the Church here and now gathered—offers in the Holy Spirit the spotless Victim to the Father. The Church's intention, however, is that the faithful not only offer this spotless Victim but also learn to offer themselves, and so day by day to be consummated, through Christ the Mediator, into unity with God and with each other, so that at last God may be all in all.

g. Intercessions: by which expression is given to the fact that the Eucharist is celebrated in communion with the entire Church, of heaven as well as of earth, and that the offering is made for her and for all her members, living and dead, who have been called to participate in the redemption and the salvation purchased by Christ's Body and Blood.

h. Final doxology: by which the glorification of God is expressed, and which is confirmed and concluded by the people's acclamation, Amen. (GIRM 79)

Notes and Comments. The Eucharistic Prayer in its many parts described above forms a single liturgical action within the course of the celebration of the Eucharist (see STL 177). The several parts of the Prayer described above suggest, by nature of their content, that they be sung. Here especially the singing of the Eucharistic Prayer in its entirety or in several of its parts gives solemn expression to the faith of the Church manifested in the text and action of this prayer. On Sundays and solemnities, especially on more solemn occasions, the priest celebrant should sing the entire Eucharistic Prayer, making use of the notations given in the *Sacramentary*: Appendix III. *Sing to the Lord* also suggests the possible singing of other compositions, that is of other tonal possibilities, approved by the USCCB for the Eucharistic Prayer (see STL 182). To date, there are no approved compositions. Given this suggestion in *Sing to the Lord*, it must be kept in mind that the chant settings already provided in the *Roman Missal*, together with the texts of the Eucharistic Prayers, form the audible translation of the text into the vernacular (see STL 181, see also GIRM 147). Thus, the need for other compositions is counter indicative to the role of prescribed chant settings in the *Roman Missal*.

On those occasions when only parts of the Eucharistic Prayer are sung as highlighted above in number 79 of the *General Instruction of the Roman Missal*, especially the Preface and its dialogue (see STL 179, see also GIRM 148), the *Sanctus*, the Anamnesis, and the Doxology (see STL 180), the parts themselves being sung determine the manner in which they are sung—an acclamation and a response to a dialogue. This differs from what is proposed in *Sing to the Lord* (see STL 178). The preface dialogue along with the preface are chanted according to the settings found in the *Sacramentary: The Order of Mass* and Appendix III. The Anamnesis, commonly called the Memorial Acclamation, and the Doxology are properly dialogues between the priest celebrant and the faithful. The responses of the faithful to the Mystery of Faith and the single Amen to the doxology are related in style and sound to the sung part of the priest celebrant. Therefore, as with all other dialogues, the musical settings already provided in the *Roman Missal* should be used. Once again, these chant settings, along with the texts, belong to the translation of these texts in the vernacular.

The *Sanctus*, which should be sung on all occasions, Sunday and weekdays, is a distinctive part of the Eucharistic Prayer. The mode chosen for singing the *Sanctus* should relate to the other parts of the Ordinary of the Mass, for example the *Gloria* and *Agnus Dei*.

The Bishops repeat the reminder in *Sing to the Lord* (see STL 182) that during the Eucharistic Prayer no other prayers or singing concur and other musical instruments should be silent except if needed to accompany the dialogues and the *Sanctus* (see STL 182, see also GIRM 32, see also RS 53).

Communion Rite

Lord's Prayer / Embolism / Doxology

What the General Instruction of the Roman Missal *Says*

> In the Lord's Prayer a petition is made for daily food, which for Christians means preeminently the eucharistic bread, and also for purification from sin, so that what is holy may, in fact, be given to those who are holy. The priest says the invitation to the prayer, and all the faithful say it with him; the priest alone adds the embolism, which the people conclude with a doxology. The embolism, enlarging upon the last petition of the Lord's Prayer itself, begs deliverance from the power of evil for the entire community of the faithful.
>
> The invitation, the Prayer itself, the embolism, and the doxology by which the people conclude these things, are sung or said aloud. (GIRM 81)

Notes and Comments. The Lord's Prayer should be sung on Sundays and solemnities. The introduction, to the Lord's Prayer, the embolism, and the doxology form a whole and when sung should be treated as such with all of these parts sung (see STL 186). The chant settings for each of these parts are found in the *Sacramentary: The Order of*

Mass. Two settings for the Lord's Prayer are provided, with one in the *Order of Mass* and the other in Appendix III.

The *General Instruction of the Roman Missal* suggests that the Lord's Prayer sung in Latin may be a valuable pastoral option (see GIRM 41).

The Rite of Peace

Notes and Comments. In *Sing to the Lord*, the Bishops do not address the importance of singing the Rite of Peace, especially the dialogue. The priest celebrant may sing the prayer, "Lord Jesus Christ," with the faithful singing the "Amen." More importantly, the priest celebrant should sing the dialogue that follows, "The peace of the Lord be with you always," with the people singing their response. When the dialogue is sung the deacon or the priest sings the invitation to offer the sign of peace. The musical settings for each of these parts are found in the *Sacramentary*: Appendix III.

The *General Instruction of the Roman Missal* and the *Order of Mass* do not foresee or allow for any sung or instrumental music as a part of the Sign of Peace. This is also indicated in *Sing to the Lord* (see STL 187). In fact, the introduction of a song or instrumental music distorts the meaning of this part of the Communion Rite with all of its other segments. The whole of the meaning of this rite is expressed in the simple gesture extended to another member of the Body of Christ without any further need for additional or confusing interpretation given by an accompanying song.

Fraction Rite/Agnus Dei

What the General Instruction of the Roman Missal *Says*

The priest breaks the Eucharistic Bread, assisted, if the case calls for it, by the deacon or a concelebrant. Christ's gesture of breaking bread at the Last Supper, which gave the entire Eucharistic Action its name in apostolic times, signifies that the many faithful are made one body (1 Corinthians 10:17) by receiving Communion from the one Bread of Life which is Christ, who died and rose for the salvation of the world. The fraction or breaking of bread is begun after the sign of peace and is carried out with proper reverence, though it should not be unnecessarily prolonged, nor should it be accorded undue importance. This rite is reserved to the priest and the deacon.

The priest breaks the Bread and puts a piece of the host into the chalice to signify the unity of the Body and Blood of the Lord in the work of salvation, namely, of the living and glorious Body of Jesus Christ. The supplication *Agnus Dei,* is, as a rule, sung by the choir or cantor with the congregation responding or it is, at least, recited aloud. This invocation accompanies the fraction and, for this reason, may be repeated as many times as necessary until the rite has reached its conclusion, the last time ending with the words dona *nobis pacem* (grant us peace). (GIRM 83)

Notes and Comments. The singing of the *Agnus Dei* should concur with the actual breaking of the bread. It begins with the breaking and concludes when this is completed. Thus, the invocation, *miserere nobis,* can be repeated as long as the breaking continues with the invocation, *dona nobis pacem,* always being the last of the invocations. The *Agnus Dei* can be carried out in a variety of ways as indicated above (see STL 188).

The *Agnus Dei* should be sung on Sundays and solemnities. The mode chosen for singing the *Agnus Dei* should relate musically to the other parts of the Ordinary of the Mass, for example, the *Gloria* and the *Sanctus.*

As with other chants in the course of the celebration of Mass, so with the *Agnus Dei,* it is not permitted to substitute other chants for those found in the Order of Mass (see GIRM 366). Therefore, the suggestion in *Sing to the Lord* that other Christological invocations besides *Agnus Dei qui tollis peccata mundi* be used is not permitted (see STL 188). Only this invocation, *Agnus Dei* or Lamb of God, acclaims fully the reality of this liturgical action as it occurs at this point in the Mass. It is the Lamb once slain who is now broken during this fraction rite for our Communion. Therefore, this sole acclamation corresponds to the whole of the Breaking of the Bread. Thus, it is this same acclaimed Lamb beheld by the assembly as we hear the invitation to Communion, *This is the Lamb of God.*

Communion Chant

What the General Instruction of the Roman Missal *Says*

While the priest is receiving the Sacrament, the Communion chant is begun. Its purpose is to express the communicants' union in spirit by means of the unity of their voices, to show joy of heart, and to highlight more clearly the "communitarian" nature of the procession to receive Communion. The singing is continued for as long as the Sacrament is being administered to the faithful. If, however, there is to be a hymn after Communion, the Communion chant should be ended in a timely manner.

Care should be taken that singers, too, can receive Communion with ease (see GIRM 86).

In the dioceses of the United States of America there are four options for the Communion chant: (1) the antiphon from the Roman Missal or the Psalm from the Roman Gradual as set to music there or in another musical setting; (2) the seasonal antiphon and Psalm of the Simple Gradual; (3) a song from another collection of psalms and antiphons, approved by the United States Conference of Catholic Bishops or the diocesan Bishop, including psalms arranged in responsorial or metrical forms; (4) a suitable liturgical song chosen in accordance with no. 86 above. This is sung either by the choir alone or by the choir or cantor with the people. (GIRM 87)

Notes and Comments.   The Communion chant begins as the priest celebrant receives Communion and continues throughout the Communion procession (see STL 189). In this way the purpose of the Communion chant to express the unity of the action of all participating in the reception of Communion with Christ and with one another is more fully expressed. Thus, the music ministers as well should receive Communion during the Communion of the faithful (see STL 195).

As with the Entrance chant and the Offertory chant, the same four options are listed for the Communion chant. Once again, the difficulty selecting from these options is the availability of approved translations and approved collections. Preference should be given to singing psalms with antiphons inspired by the proper texts in the *Graduale Romanum* or the seasonal text in the *Graduale Simplex* (see STL 190, 192, 194). The choice is often times option four, a suitable liturgical song, which may be inspired by the Gospel of the day or the action of eating and drinking the Body and Blood of the Lord (see STL 191).

The Communion chant, which should be a single chant corresponding to the one procession and the unity of the action of communion in Christ, can be sung by all or by the choir alone (see STL 189). *Sing to the Lord* suggests that more than one chant be sung during the Communion procession if it is lengthy (see STL 193). Such a suggestion might at first appear practical, but, in the end, compromises the significant unity of the procession regardless of its length rendered with a single song. When one of the first three options for the Communion chant is planned, it is possible with a skilled accompanist to adapt the chant, that is, the psalm and its antiphon, to correspond to the length of the procession. When the fourth option is planned, it is possible to include musical interludes drawn from the liturgical song which will help serve the length of the procession. In any case, the singing of the Communion chant resolves with the end of the Communion procession.

Hymn of Praise

What the General Instruction of the Roman Missal *Says*

> When the distribution of Communion is finished, as circumstances suggest, the priest and faithful spend some time praying privately. If desired, a psalm or other canticle of praise or a hymn may also be sung by the entire congregation. (GIRM 88)

Notes and Comments.   The period that follows the reception of Holy Communion is typically observed with a corporate silence, a silence engaged in by the priest and faithful for prayer. The focus of this prayer is on the mysteries just received, the Body and Blood of the Lord. In the same way, if a psalm or hymn is sung, this should be carried out by all and the focus remains on the mysteries just received (see STL 196). No specific title or name for this sung psalm or hymn is given in the *General Instruction* or *Order of Mass*. It seems best to call it just what it is—a Psalm of Praise or a Hymn of Praise. Little direction on this psalm or hymn is provided in the *General Instruction of the Roman Missal* or even in the *Order of Mass*. However, when choices are made to sing at this period both the relationship of the

piece to the whole liturgical assembly and the purpose of the song
should be kept in mind. The *General Instruction*, to give further
emphasis to this song being an action of the whole liturgical assembly,
directs that the assembly may stand during this period and sing.
It would be incorrect to call this song a Meditation Hymn; since it is
not for or on behalf of the assembly but the corporate response of those
who have just received the Sacrament. Also, given the purpose for this
song, likewise, Marian antiphons and hymns would be inappropriate.

Prayer after Communion

Notes and Comments.   The Prayer after Communion and the
"Amen" of the faithful should be sung on Sundays and Solemnities.
Sample tones are found in the *Missale Romanum*: Appendix I: *Cantus
varii in ordine Missae occurrentes*, and the *Sacramentary*, Appendix III:
The Order of Mass.

   The Bishops again suggest in *Sing to the Lord* that, like the
other presidential prayers, only the conclusion may be sung along with
the "Amen" of the faithful (see STL 197). This suggestion, as already
treated above with the Collect, fails to account for the integrity of
the whole of the prayer when it separates out some of its parts for song
over others.

Concluding Rite

Notes and Comments.   The Concluding Rite consists of the greeting,
blessing, and dismissal. During certain liturgical seasons and
observances a Prayer over the People or Solemn Blessing may be used
(see GIRM 90b, 167). On Sundays and solemnities all of the parts
of the Concluding Rite should be sung (see STL 198). The chant for
each of these parts can be found in the *Sacramentary*: Appendix III.
When the priest celebrant sings the greeting and blessing then the
deacon sings the dismissal. During the whole of the Easter Octave
and Pentecost Sunday the double alleluia according to the chant form
provided in the *Roman Missal* should be sung.

Hymn after Mass

Notes and Comments. The *General Instruction of the Roman Missal* and the *Order of Mass* do not mention anything about music or song following the dismissal. However, according to the U.S. Bishops, it is a custom in the United States for music or song to take place at this time (see STL 199). The possibilities are quite varied from a piece carried out by the choir alone, a schola, or the whole liturgical assembly as well as instrumental music of a great variety (see STL 199). *Sing to the Lord* proposes something other than a congregational piece in those instances when a song follows Communion (see STL 199).

Choices for the recessional should be in accord with what we have already been presented in this book on what is appropriate music or song for the celebration of the Sacred Liturgy as well as for the liturgical season or observance. The hymn after Mass may also be an occasion to sing a Marian hymn or, at times, a patriotic song as long as such a choice, a choice again appropriate for a sacred occasion, does not obscure the celebration of a particular Sunday or solemnity. *Sing to the Lord* lists silence as an appropriate option especially during Lent (see STL 199).

What about Silence during the Celebration of the Sacred Liturgy?

At this point it is necessary to treat the topic of silence in the course of the celebration of the Sacred Liturgy. In fact, silence is a part of the celebration of the Eucharist as seen above and will also be seen in the discussion of the other liturgical rites in the subsequent chapters.

What the General Instruction of the Roman Missal *says*

> Sacred silence also, as part of the celebration, is to be observed at the designated times. Its purpose, however, depends on the time it occurs in each part of the celebration. Thus within the Act of Penitence and again after the invitation to pray, all recollect themselves; but at the conclusion of a reading or the homily, all meditate briefly on what they have heard; then after Communion, they praise and pray to God in their hearts.
>
> Even before the celebration itself, it is commendable that silence be observed in the church, in the sacristy, in the vesting room, and in adjacent

areas, so that all may dispose themselves to carry out the sacred action in a devout and fitting manner (GIRM 45).

Notes and Comments.   Silence is not the absence of a spoken text or liturgical music. Rather, as indicated by the *General Instruction,* it is a corporate act on the part of the liturgical assembly which occurs at varying moments during the liturgical celebration. Silence allows for all to recollect or meditate or to praise God with one another in the unfolding of the Sacred Mysteries. As the *Order of Mass* assigns certain times for liturgical silence so it will be seen in the other liturgical rites, and for similar reasons. Silence also gives the liturgical assembly the opportunity to more fully take in the benefits of liturgical music.

CONCLUSION

We have examined how we sing the Eucharist. For the most part, our sources have been the *Roman Missal* and its general instruction, focusing our attention on the sung Ordinary and Proper of the Mass. The theological and liturgical principles highlighted in this chapter help us to understand with these same principles how to sing the other Sacraments presented in the next chapter.

Chapter 7

How Do We Sing the Other Sacraments?

INTRODUCTION

All of the ritual books for the celebration of the Sacraments, as in the *Roman Missal*, provide texts and chants for the celebration of these same Sacraments. While it states in *Sing to the Lord* that these texts and chants are not mandatory, they indicate what should be sung so the pastor or liturgical music minister will see what is appropriate music for the rites (see STL 200). In this chapter, we will review these ritual books in order to see what the Church proposes for texts and chants proper to the celebration of each Sacrament. Many of the proposed texts in the sacramental rituals do not have an accompanying chant. The chant forms, however, in the *Roman Missal* for the greetings and presidential prayers guide the priest celebrant and the faithful in sacramental celebrations. *Sing to the Lord* contains a generic overview of singing the Sacraments while this book is more comprehensive and relies on the liturgical books for the examples of what to sing.

Oftentimes the choice of what to sing during a sacramental celebration will have the descriptor, "appropriate" or "suitable." You will recall the previous explanation of these terms in the introduction to Chapter 6. An "appropriate" or "suitable" song is measured by the ritual occasion, the example of proposed texts, both what the text says and the nature of the text, and the musical capacity of those singing. The purpose of this companion is to endorse and support STL in the singing of the given liturgical texts. When other suitable songs must be prepared, then the guidance provided in Chapter 5 of this companion should be followed.

In the previous chapter, the general principles that we discussed for the singing of the Liturgy of the Word should also be applied to a Liturgy of the Word in a sacramental celebration. Even when the structure and norms for a Liturgy of the Word in a sacramental celebration vary from those of the Mass, the principles for singing remain the same. You will notice that the liturgical books and rites for all of the Sacraments and some other sacramental celebrations include a lectionary. This lectionary is often only a listing of the biblical texts rather than a book itself.

As always, singing the Sacred Liturgy in the celebration of the Sacraments forms the priest and faithful in their actual participation in the Mysteries of the Lord. Pastors and liturgical musicians should make every effort to ensure that singing takes place in these celebrations as well as in the many rites that belong to the Order of each of the Sacraments. This will be illustrated below.

The review of the Sacraments in this Chapter follows the order listed in the *Catechism of the Catholic Church*, Sacraments of Initiation, Sacraments of Healing, and Sacraments at the Service of Communion. *Sing to the Lord*, in its survey of the Sacraments lists the Sacraments at the Service of Communion before the Sacraments of Healing.

We need to recall what has already been discussed as to why we sing, how singing fosters our interior participation, and highlights theological dimensions of the liturgical celebration. If we are typically singing the Eucharist well, and with Sunday singing as our norm, then both for clergy and faithful, singing the Sacraments should also soon become the norm. It is important then to provide musicians and aids to singing for sacramental celebrations. It is also important to become comfortable with unaccompanied singing in sacramental celebrations (see STL 207). This approach to singing the Sacraments, guided by *Sing to the Lord*, will be a new challenge for many of us as pastors and liturgical musicians, especially in the case of singing at Sunday Baptisms and considering what should be sung at Marriages. This is a liturgical musical challenge worth its efforts!

THE SACRAMENTS OF INITIATION

What Should We Sing during the Rite of Christian Initiation of Adults?

Each of the steps and periods of the Christian initiation of adults includes parts and occasions marked by liturgical music. *Sing to the Lord* provides us only a cursory look at each of these same steps and periods for liturgical music. In this section, using *Sing to the Lord* as a guide, we will look at the rites of the Christian initiation of adults in greater detail with an emphasis on all of the sung parts.

   Singing the Sacred Liturgy is one of the chief ways to form the Christian community in the faith and also one of the chief ways the Christian community helps to form catechumens as well. Pastors and music ministers should be mindful to provide this liturgical musical formation for catechumens when they are gathered with the whole liturgical assembly and when they gather in small groups as a means of faith formation (see STL 202). Perhaps the introduction of liturgical music to the catechumens may be gradual; however, it never should be lacking.

What Should We Sing during the Rite of Acceptance into the Order of Catechumens?

The Rite of Acceptance into the Order of Catechumens often takes place at a Sunday Mass with due regard for the liturgical season or observance. During the Reception of the Candidates, which takes place at or near the entrance of the church, the faithful may sing a psalm or an appropriate song (see STL 203).[1] If this rite occurs with Mass then the options for the Entrance chant for the Mass of the day should be considered. After the Greeting of the celebrant and before the Opening Dialogue an appropriate song, for example, Psalm 63:1–8, may be sung.[2] With both the A and B option for the Signing of the Candidates with the Cross, the acclamation is better sung than recited (see STL 203).[3] Following the Invitation to the Celebration of the Word of God and during the procession where the Liturgy of the Word will be celebrated, an appropriate song is sung

---

1. See RCIA 48.
2. See RCIA 49.
3. See RCIA 54–56.

(see STL 203) or the following antiphon, "Come, my children, listen to me; I will teach you the fear of the Lord", with Psalm 34:2, 3, 6, 9, 10, 11, 16.[4] When the Rite of Acceptance into the Order of Catechumens takes place apart from Mass, the Dismissal of the Catechumens may be followed by an appropriate song while keeping in mind the liturgical season or observance.[5]

What Should We Sing during the Rites Belonging to the Period of the Catechumenate?

The period of the catechumenate can last, depending on a great variety of circumstances, anywhere from one to three years. These are the liturgical rites that belong to this period:
- Celebrations of the Word of God;[6]
- Minor Exorcisms;[7]
- Blessings of the Catechumens;[8] and
- Anointing of the Catechumens.[9]

The Celebration of the Word of God many times includes the minor exorcisms, blessings, and anointings. The Model for a Celebration of the Word of God suggests an appropriate song to open the celebration.[10] A sung responsorial psalm should follow each reading.[11] With this celebration of the Word of God, the catechumens are introduced to the formative role of singing the Liturgy and are thus instructed to more fully participate in singing the Sunday Eucharist.

What Should We Sing during the Rite of Election or Enrollment of Names?

This rite, which usually takes place with the Diocesan Bishop on the First Sunday of Lent, again follows the norms for singing a Liturgy of the Word. With the Invitation and Enrollment of Names, as the enrollment is taking place, an appropriate song may be sung (see STL 204),

---

4. See RCIA 60.
5. See RCIA 67D.
6. See RCIA 81–89.
7. See RCIA 90–94.
8. See RCIA 95–97.
9. See RCIA 98–103.
10. See RCIA 86.
11. See RCIA 87.

for example, Psalm 16 or 33 with an antiphon such as "Happy the people the Lord has chosen to be his own."[12] With the Rite of Election or Enrollment of Names, the Dismissal of the Elect may conclude with an appropriate song keeping in mind the liturgical season or observance.[13]

What Should We Sing during the Scrutinies?

The Scrutinies typically occur on the Third, Fourth, and Fifth Sundays of Lent, making use of the Cycle A readings from the *Lectionary*. Following the Exorcism at each Scrutiny an appropriate song may be sung (see STL 205), for example, Psalm 6, 26, 32, 38, 39, 40, 51, 116:1–9, 130, 139, or 142.[14]

What Should We Sing during the Presentation of the Creed and the Lord's Prayer?

The presentation of the Creed typically occurs during the week after the First Scrutiny and the presentation of the Lord's Prayer during the week after the Third Scrutiny. When these presentations occur outside of Mass the norms for singing a Liturgy of the Word are followed and, with the Dismissal of the Elect, an appropriate song may conclude the celebration.[15]

What Should We Sing during the Preparation Rites on Holy Saturday?

The Model for a Celebration of the Preparation Rites indicates that a suitable song opens the celebration.[16] The norms for singing a Liturgy of the Word are followed. Again, a suitable psalm or hymn may be sung between the readings.[17]

What Should We Sing during the Celebration of the Sacraments of Initiation (Easter Vigil)?

With the Celebration of Baptism, the Litany of the Saints is sung (see STL 206). The Litany is sung by the deacon or cantor or choir

---

12. See RCIA 132.
13. See RCIA 136 D.
14. See RCIA 154, 168, 175.
15. See RCIA 162D and 183D.
16. See RCIA 187.
17. See RCIA 189.

with the faithful responding. The given form and content of the Litany for those to be baptized is found in the ritual book. Additional names of saints, that is, canonized saints only, and appropriate petitions may be included with special attention to the proper place for their insertion in the litany.[18] The litanic form of this supplication is constitutive of this rite, the Litany of the Saints. It should not be arbitrarily set aside in favor of a hymn or song; nor should its unique form and specified content be set aside.

With the Prayer over the Water, the faithful sing the acclamation, "Springs of water, bless the Lord. Give him glory and praise for ever" or another suitable acclamation (see STL 206).[19]

With the Baptism, if a large number of adults are to be baptized, the faithful may sing during the Sacrament.[20] Typically, however, the number of adults to be baptized is small and after each Baptism a short acclamation may be sung (see STL 206).[21] Appendix II, number 595, of the ritual book *Rite of Christian Initiation of Adults* provides twelve possible acclamations from Sacred Scripture.

With the Celebration of Confirmation, the faithful may sing a suitable song between the Baptism and Confirmation (see STL 206).[22] *Sing to the Lord* recommends a possible song during the Confirmation of the neophytes, especially if the number is large (see STL 206).[23] With the Renewal of Baptismal Promises at the Easter Vigil, as the priest celebrant sprinkles all the people with the blessed baptismal water, all sing the following song or any other that is baptismal in character:

I saw water flowing
from the right side of the temple, alleluia.
It brought God's life and his salvation,
and the people sang in joyful praise:
alleluia, alleluia. (See Ezekiel 47:1–2, 9)[24]

---

18. See RCIA 221.
19. See RCIA 222.
20. See RCIA 226.
21. See RCIA 226; see also Appendix II.
22. See RCIA 231.
23. See RCIA 235.
24. See RCIA 240.

What Should We Sing during the *Rite of Baptism for Children*?

The celebration of the Sacrament of Baptism for Children takes place at the Easter Vigil, Easter Sunday, and the Sundays throughout the year. The Sacrament of Baptism may be celebrated within Mass to show the relationship between Baptism and the Eucharist but not too frequently (see STL 211).[25] The celebration of the Sacrament of Baptism should take place at a common celebration on the same day. Thus, Baptism should not be celebrated more than once on the same day in the same church.[26] It seems preferable because of the relation of Baptism to the Eucharist that, when the sacrament is celebrated apart from Mass, it should precede Mass instead of follow it. Baptism as the occasion for forming many members into the single Body of Christ and its completion in the Eucharist is the reason for the directive that it occur only once a day and that it be celebrated, when apart from Mass, before Mass. In this way, many more of the faithful could likely attend the Baptism since they will already be gathering for the Eucharist.

There are several rites outlined in the ritual book for the Baptism for children. The most common form is the Rite of Baptism for Several Children which is illustrated for singing below. When Baptism is celebrated within Mass those pertinent parts of the celebration intended to be sung outside of Mass are also sung during Mass (see STL 212).

What the Rite of Baptism for Children *Says*

> The celebration of baptism is greatly enhanced by the use of song. It stimulates a sense of unity among those present, it gives warmth to their common prayer, it expresses the joy of Easter. Conferences of bishops should encourage and help musical specialists to compose settings for texts suitable for congregational singing at baptism.[27]

---

25. See RBC 9.

26. See RBC, Christian Initiation, General Introduction, 27.

27. RBC, Christian Initiation, General Introduction, 33.

What Should We Sing during the Rite of Baptism for Several Children?

Each of the segments of the Rite of Baptism for Several Children includes parts to be sung. Singing these parts, with the encouragement of the celebrant and the assistance of music ministers, will help all to enter more deeply into the Mystery of Christ celebrated in Baptism. Of course, these celebrations of the rite will require more preparation. Music ministers will have to be in place and the ritual requirements coordinated with liturgical music planning.

What Should We Sing during the Reception of the Children?

The assembled parents, godparents, and others may sing a psalm or suitable song for the occasion of Baptism as the priest or deacon processes to meet them at the entrance of the church or wherever the assembly has gathered (see STL 208).[28] After the signing of each child's forehead the celebrant invites the parents, godparents, and others to participate in the Liturgy of the Word. During the procession to the ambo or place where this will be celebrated a song is sung, for example, Psalm 85:7, 8, 9ab whose text is found in Appendix I, 1, of the *Rite of Baptism for Children* (see STL 208).[29]

What Should We Sing during the Celebration of God's Word?

The norms stated earlier for singing the Liturgy of the Word apply with these additions as noted in the Rite of Baptism for Children. After the homily or in the course of or after the litany, it is desirable to have a period of silence while all pray at the celebrant's invitation. If convenient, a suitable song follows this silence (see STL 209), for example, those songs found in *Chapter VII, Various Texts for Use in the Celebration of Baptism for Children*, 225–245.[30]

If possible, the Prayer of the Faithful and the invocation of the saints should be sung using the melodies found in the *Roman Missal*.[31] In the case of the celebration of Baptism, the celebrant sings the litany.[32] As the parents and godparents with the children process

---

28. See RBC 35.
29. See RBC 42.
30. See RBC 46.
31. See Sacramentary: Easter Vigil 41.
32. See RBC 48.

to the place of Baptism, if convenient, a suitable song may be sung, for example, Psalm 23, whose text is found in Appendix I, 2 in the Rite of Baptism for Children (see STL 209).[33]

What Should We Sing during the Celebration of the Sacrament?

The Blessing and Invocation of God over Baptismal Water, as one of the principal presidential prayers during the rite, should be sung by the celebrant as well as the faithful's, "Amen." Several forms are provided for this blessing. Forms B and C include an acclamation or the possibility of another suitable acclamation, both of which should be sung.

The Profession of Faith concludes with the assent "This is our faith," which can be put aside in favor of some other formula or a suitable song. The faithful sings this song expressing their faith with a single voice (see STL 209).[34] If a suitable song is chosen, its role as the assent of the faithful should be considered as well as length and text.

After the Baptism of each child the people may sing a short acclamation using, for example, one of the songs found in *Chapter VII, Various Texts for Use in the Celebration of Baptism for Children*, 225–245 (see STL 209).[35]

What Should We Sing during the Conclusion of the Rite?

For the conclusion of the rite and when there is a procession to the altar, a suitable baptismal song may be sung (see STL 210), for example:

> You have put on Christ,
> in him you have been baptized.
> Alleluia, alleluia.[36]

Other songs may be sung as found in Chapter VII, "Various Texts for Use in the Celebration of Baptism for Children," 225–245.[37]

After the blessing and dismissal, a suitable song may be sung expressing thanksgiving and Easter joy or the *Magnificat* may be sung (see STL 210).[38]

---

33. See RBC 52.
34. See RBC 59.
35. See RBC 60.
36. See RBC 67.
37. See RBC 67.
38. See RBC 71

What Should We Sing during the *Rite of Confirmation for Children*?

The celebration of the Sacrament of Confirmation for children, a celebration which usually coincides with the parochial visit of the Bishop as the ordinary minister of the sacrament, provides an occasion for a solemn celebration of the Eucharist (see STL 213). The Sacrament of Confirmation may be administered outside of Mass and this form as well calls for great solemnity with singing the pertinent parts of the Liturgy of the Word and of the Rite of Confirmation (see STL 215). The Sacred Liturgy with the Bishop is the primordial celebration of the Church and this of itself calls for song throughout the course of the rites.

The Sacrament of Confirmation for children typically takes place on Sunday during Easter time. When it is celebrated at other times, due regard must be given to the liturgical season and observance. What has been said above concerning the solemn celebration of Mass, especially with a Bishop, should be observed for the celebration of the Sacrament of Confirmation (see STL 213).

What the Rite of Confirmation *Says*

Renewal of Baptismal Promises

> After the homily the candidates stand and the bishop questions them: . . . For "This is our faith," some other formula may be substituted, or the community may express its faith in a suitable song.[39]

The Laying on of Hands

> The concelebrating priests stand near the bishop. He faces the people and with hands joined, sings or says: "My dear friends . . . ."
> The bishop and the priests who will minister the sacrament with him lay hands upon all the candidates (by extending their hands over them). The bishop alone sings or says: "All-powerful God . . . ."[40]

---

39. RC 23.
40. RC 23 and 24.

The Anointing with Chrism

During the anointing a suitable song may be song.[41]

Notes and Comments.   When "This is our faith" is put aside in favor
of some other formula or a suitable song, the choice for the Profession
of Faith in the *Rite of Baptism for Children* would be appropriate
for this celebration of the Sacrament of Confirmation.[42] This establishes
an important association of the profession of faith in the initiation
sacraments of Baptism and Confirmation. If a suitable song is chosen,
its role as the assent of the faithful should be part of the consideration
as well as length and text. The candidates themselves are to sing
this assent.

The Invitation to Prayer and the Prayer itself during the
laying on of hands, as one of the principal presidential prayers during
the rite as well as the faithful's "Amen" should be sung by the Bishop
as a manifestation of the solemnity of this action of the Holy Spirit.

The Anointing with Chrism is a single action by the Bishop
(and priests who may be associated with him for this anointing)
accompanied by song or silence. For this reason, although *Sing to the
Lord* suggests singing one or more songs, and even identifying as a
possible hymn, *Veni Creator Spiritus* (see STL 214), even when a large
number is to be confirmed, it is better to accompany the anointing
with a song and, in this case, a single song. This song may be a psalm
with an antiphon or a suitable song that expresses the action that
is taking place.

What Should We Sing During the *Reception of First Holy Communion for Children?*

For the sake of completeness, we would like to introduce a few points
to keep in mind for the reception of First Holy Communion as part
of this brief review of singing the Sacraments of Initiation.

The reception of First Communion typically occurs within
the celebration of the Sunday Mass during Easter time. Circular
Letter *Paschale Solemnitatis,* On Preparing and Celebrating the Paschal
Feasts (1988), suggests the appropriateness of the Fourth Sunday of

---

41. RC 29.
42. See RBC 59.

Easter, for first Communion.[43] What is said above about singing the Eucharist guides and should govern these celebrations of the reception of First Communion.

The Sacraments of Healing

What Should We Sing During the *Rite of Penance*?

The communal celebration of the Rite of Penance provides a unique pastoral occasion for the choice of liturgical music to give a clearer context for the texts and the action of Christ and the Church in this Sacrament. The following introductory material in the *Rite of Penance* directs the celebration of the *Rite for Reconciliation of Several Penitents*.

What the Rite of Penance *Says*

> When the faithful are assembled, a suitable hymn may be sung. Then the priest greets them, and, if necessary, he or another minister gives a brief introduction to the celebration and explains the order of service. Next, he invites all to pray and after a period of silence completes the (opening) prayer. . . . At the invitation of the deacon or other minister, all kneel or bow their heads and say a form of general confession (for example, I confess to almighty God). Then they stand and join in a litany or suitable song to express confession of sins, heartfelt contrition, prayer for forgiveness, and trust in God's mercy. Finally, they say the Lord's Prayer, which is never omitted . . . .
>
> When the confessions are over, the priests return to the sanctuary. The priest who presides invites all to make an act of thanksgiving and to praise God for his mercy. This may be done in a psalm or hymn or litany. Finally, the priest concludes the celebration with prayer, praising God for the great love he has shown us. (RP 23, 27, 29)

Notes and Comments.

The celebration outlined in Chapter Two of the Rite of Penance, Reconciliation of Several Penitents with Individual Confession and Absolution, begins with a psalm, antiphon or other appropriate song while the priest enters the church (see STL 229).[44] Examples are provided in the ritual book which may inspire choices

---

43. Circular Letter *Paschale Solemnitatis* (PS), On Preparing and Celebrating the Paschal Feasts (1988), 103.

44. See RP 48, 23.

for this song, keeping in mind the liturgical season or observance. The Liturgy of the Word should be planned according to the liturgical musical norms already described above (see STL 229). During the rite of reconciliation, that is, the general confession of sins, this general confession is followed by a litany or an appropriate song (see STL 229).[45] The proclamation of praise for God's mercy belongs to the complete celebration of this rite (see STL 229). When individual confessions are concluded, "[I]t is fitting for all to sing a psalm or hymn or to say a litany in acknowledgment of God's power and mercy, for example, the canticle of Mary (Luke 1:46–55) or Psalm 136:1–9, 13–14, 16, 25–26."[46] Other examples of the proclamation of praise are found in "Chapter Four: Various Texts Used in the Celebration of Reconciliation."

In Appendix II of *The Rite of Penance* there are "*Sample Penitential Services,*" which do not include sacramental confession but rather foster the spirit and virtue of penance. These services also should include song when it is indicated and appropriate to that part of the celebration, keeping in mind the liturgical season or observance.

Sing to the Lord suggests an optional hymn after the homily (see STL 229). However, the *Rite of Penance* promotes corporate silence after the homily for the examination of conscience so as to awaken true contrition for sin.[47] The hymn that follows this belongs to the next part of the rite, the general confession of sins. *Sing to the Lord* suggests that "[s]inging or soft instrumental music may be used during the time of individual confessions, especially when a large number is present for the celebration" (see STL 229).

"Chapter Two: Rite for Reconciliation of Several Penitents with Individual Confession and Absolution" is frequently the form used for the celebration of the first confession of school age children. What is noted above about the use of song in this rite applies also to these celebrations for children.

---

45. See RP 54, 27.
46. RP 56; see RP 29.
47. See RP 26.

What Should We Sing during the *Pastoral Care of the Sick?*

Rites of Anointing and Viaticum

As in the *Rite of Penance*, liturgical music gives a clearer context for the texts and action of Christ and the Church in the Sacrament. This point is made as well in the introduction to the *Pastoral Care of the Sick: Rites of Anointing and Viaticum:*

> The full participation of those present must be fostered by every means, especially through the use of appropriate songs, so that the celebration manifests the Easter joy which is proper to this sacrament [see STL 227]. (PCS 108)

Anointing outside Mass

Notes and Comments.   If this form for the celebration of the Sacrament of the Sick occurs with a large group of people, there should be song. The celebration opens with an appropriate psalm or hymn, again with a choice that reflects the liturgical season or observance. The Sprinkling with Holy Water may be accompanied by a chant similar to those sung when this rite occurs during Mass. The Litany and the Prayer over the Oil may also be sung with responses easily made by the faithful (see STL 228). If Communion is distributed, a suitable psalm or hymn should be sung. The celebration may conclude with an appropriate song.[48]

Silence should accompany the Laying on of Hands.[49] However, during the Anointing, "[a]fter the sacramental form has been heard at least once by those present, suitable songs may be sung while the rest of the sick are being anointed."[50] Silence during the laying of hands in the Sacrament of the Sick serves the same purpose as when it accompanies this same ritual action in other Sacraments. The silence is corporate and participative with all in reverent communion with the Holy Spirit who brings about the work of Christ. Also, even with what is said in the *Pastoral Care of the Sick* and *Sing to the Lord*, the unity of the action during the anointing is better expressed when only one psalm or song accompanies it. The Bishops'

---

48. See PCS 109.
49. See PCS 122.
50. PCS 110.

recommendation in *Sing to the Lord* that instrumental music might accompany the anointing lacks the level of participation that is achieved even with silence over singing (see STL 228).

Anointing within Mass

Notes and Comments.   This celebration may take place in either a large group or with only a few participants. The celebration may occur in a church or in another suitable setting. What has been said above regarding singing and the celebration of the Sacrament of the Sick applies also when it occurs during Mass. However, as far as those parts of the Mass to be sung with the Anointing of the Sick, the norms and guidelines for singing the Eucharist should be observed (see STL 228). Special attention once again should be given to the liturgical season or observance.

In both celebrations of the Anointing outside of Mass and within Mass, a part of the necessary and proper preparation of the Sacred Liturgy is song provided with an organist/instrumentalist, leader of song, psalmist, or choir or schola.

THE SACRAMENTS AT THE SERVICE OF COMMUNION

What Should We Sing during the *Order of Celebrating Marriage?*

In *Sing to the Lord*, the U.S. Bishops refer to the provisional English translation of the second Latin edition of the *Order of Celebrating Marriage* when it discusses liturgical music and the celebration of this Sacrament.[51] Much of what is described in the current *Rite of Marriage* with regard to singing is also found in this anticipated new translation, the *Order of Celebrating Marriage.*

> The songs chosen should be appropriate to the celebration of the rite of marriage and express the faith of the Church; due regard is to be given to the importance of the responsorial psalm within the Liturgy of the

---

51. *Order of Celebrating Marriage,* Second Typical Edition, from the Roman Ritual, revised by decree of the Second Vatican Council published by authority of Pope Paul VI revised at the direction of Pope John Paul II. Unpublished English Translation, ICEL, Washington, DC, 1996.

Word. What applies to songs applies also to the choice of other musical compositions. (OCM 30)

Notes and Comments.   Number 30 above in the *General Introduction to the Order of Celebrating Marriage* restates the nature of liturgical music and, in this case, for the Sacrament of Marriage, what is appropriate to the rite and expressive of the faith of the Church (see STL 217). What has been described above concerning the singing of the Eucharist should be observed in the preparation of all of the liturgical music for the celebration of Marriage within Mass. This is especially true for the Liturgy of the Word (see STL 222). Additionally, the liturgical music planned should be inclusive of the liturgical season or observance when the Marriage is celebrated, especially in the privileged seasons, Sundays, and solemnities. *Secular music, even if it promotes Christian sentiment with regard to Marriage, is out of place in the celebration of Marriage.*

As pastors and liturgical musicians, we all know the many questions and concerns that surround preparing for the celebration of the Sacrament of Marriage. Oftentimes the aim of promoting a correspondence between the sung faith in liturgical music choices and the desires of the bride and groom can be quite the challenge. We need to be active in our presentation and planning with the bride and groom, outlining ideas and suggestions according to what is described below. This will help the couple achieve a correspondence between both what the Church requires for singing the Sacrament of Marriage and their own particular choices.

What Should We Sing during Marriage within Mass?

The *Order of Celebrating Marriage* describes as part of the Introductory Rites two ways to receive the bride and bridegroom.

A. Reception at the Door of the Church
At the appointed time, the priest, vested in an alb and a stole and chasuble of the color of the Mass to be celebrated, goes with the ministers to the door of the church. There he receives the couple and greets them in a warm and friendly manner, showing that the Church shares their joy.

The procession to the altar then takes place: the ministers go first, followed by the priest, and the couple. According to local custom, they may be accompanied by at least their parents and the two witnesses to the place prepared for them. Meanwhile, the opening song is sung. (OCM 48)

B. Reception at a Place within the Church

At the appointed time, the priest, vested in an alb and a stole and chasuble of the color of the Mass to be celebrated, goes with the ministers to the place prepared for the couple or to the chair.

When the couple comes to their place, the priest receives them and greets them in a warm and friendly manner, showing that the Church shares their joy. Then the opening song is sung. (OCM 49)

Notes and Comments.   What has already been described in this book concerning the Entrance chant at Mass applies also to Mass with the Sacrament of Marriage. This chant, in addition to its role to accompany the procession, also introduces the mystery to be celebrated. Therefore, the choice for the opening song in both of the forms of the reception of the bride and bridegroom should express either the liturgical observance if the Wedding Mass is not used, for example, on certain Sundays and solemnities, or the mystery of marriage when the Wedding Mass is used. When the Wedding Mass is used, the texts provided in the *Graduale Romanum*, the *Graduale Simplex*, or the antiphons for recitation for the Wedding Masses in the *Roman Missal* might inspire choices for other psalms and suitable liturgical songs. In this way, the opening song for the *Order of Christian Marriage* is in accord with the American Bishops' adaptation to the *General Instruction of the Roman Missal* for the Entrance chant at Mass.

The U.S. Bishops' general recommendation in *Sing to the Lord* is that the entrance procession should be accompanied by a suitable song or instrumental music, and if instrumental music is played then the assembly may join in a song once all have taken their places. This recommendation fails to note the significance of form A (see STL 222). When form A, as described above, is used, the priest and ministers of the Sacrament of Marriage process to the altar. This is the liturgical procession for the Mass; the Entrance chant should express the mystery of the liturgical observance or marriage. When form B is used, with the priest meeting the ministers of the Sacrament of Marriage at another place or at the chair, instrumental music may accompany the procession of the bride and groom with the Entrance chant occurring after the priest greets them.

What has already been described in this book concerning the Communion chant at Mass applies also to Mass with the Sacrament of Marriage. Again, what was just stated above as far as sources for the Communion chant when Marriage is celebrated within Mass also applies.

Following the *Reception of the Consent* there is an *Acclamation of Praise* which could be the following, "Let us bless the Lord," or another acclamation to which the people respond, "Thanks be to God."[52] As with similar acclamations, this also could be sung.

Following the *Exchange of Rings,* there is the possibility of singing a hymn or a song of praise.[53] This *Song of Praise,* as in other instances in the Roman Rite, should refer to the mystery just celebrated, namely the Sacrament of Marriage.

The order for the celebration of the Sacrament of Marriage outside of Mass includes the same two possible forms as described above. Although Mass will not be celebrated, the choice for the opening song should be suited to accompany the procession and introduce the mystery of the Sacrament of Marriage. The *Celebration of Marriage* is the same whether within or outside of Mass (see STL 223).

Marriage outside Mass can also include Holy Communion with an accompanying chant followed by a song of praise (see STL 223). In this case, the choice for the Communion chant corresponds to the outline of options used for Communion during Mass. The choice for the *Song of Praise* that may follow should likewise correspond to the directives for such a song in the celebration of Mass. The *Song of Praise* should refer to the mystery just received.

There are some additional points not discussed in *Sing to the Lord* that should be mentioned.

Sign of Peace

The sign of peace expresses the peace of Christ already present among those celebrating the Eucharist. The option to exchange the sign of peace after the priest's greeting signifies the peace and communion among those who will soon participate in the Eucharistic Body of

52. OCM 61.
53. See OCM 64.

Christ. The sign of peace is intended to be a simple, noble, and clear gesture shared only with those near one another. There should be no liturgical music of any kind, instrumental or sung, to accompany the sign of peace.

The sign of peace belongs to the Communion Rite since its meaning is derived from its place in anticipation of Eucharistic Communion. Therefore, the sign of peace takes place only when Marriage is celebrated within Mass and when Holy Communion follows Marriage outside Mass. There is no sign of peace during Marriage outside Mass unless it includes the reception of Communion.

Prayer at the Marian Altar or Shrine

The practice of the bride and bridegroom visiting the Marian altar or shrine following the celebration of the sacrament of Marriage should reflect sincere devotion to Mary, the Mother of the Lord. The *Order for Celebrating Marriage*, as well as *Sing to the Lord*, makes no reference to this devotional practice; therefore, if it does take place, it should occur after the Concluding Rite.

Notes and Comments.   For many pastors and liturgical music ministers, weddings often prove to be challenges to carry out authentically all that has been stated about the celebration of the Sacrament. We can meet this challenge in pastorally creative and careful ways when we hold to the importance of liturgical norms in this Sacrament as in the celebration of the others (see STL 217). Couples, as well as pastors and liturgical music ministers, must recall that the liturgical rites for marriage are for celebrations of the Church and not private or personal celebrations. To keep this balance and, recognizing all of the cultural and social issues surrounding weddings, pastors and liturgical music ministers should be supportive of couples with "pastoral sensitivity and sound judgment" (see STL 217).

Pastors and liturgical music ministers will be greatly assisted in their roles and duties if diocesan and parish guidelines are in place and well known when helping couples prepare for the celebration of the Sacrament of Marriage. These guidelines better serve the couple when they are part of their initial contact with the clergy when making arrangements for the wedding (see STL 119). As with the choice and planning of music for all the Sacraments, it is especially the case with Marriage that the three judgments given in *Sing to the Lord* are employed. The U.S. Bishops add, ". . . music should reflect the truth that all the sacraments celebrate the Paschal Mystery of Christ.[54] Secular music, even though it may emphasize the love of the spouses for one another, is not appropriate for the Sacred Liturgy. Songs that are chosen for the Liturgy should be appropriate for the celebration and express the faith of the Church"[55] (STL 220).

The liturgical music ministers serving the celebration of Marriage should know the liturgical rites and norms for the Order of Christian Marriage. Oftentimes the parish Sunday liturgical music ministers are most suited to serve at weddings. When soloists or vocalists are employed to assist with the wedding music, all that we have discussed previously concerning the role of the cantor or psalmist, their duties and placement, along with regard for what we should sing during the Eucharist and Marriage, must be respected (see STL 221). The liturgical assembly and the couple themselves will be assisted in their own participation when printed aids to the celebration, with special attention to the rite of marriage, are provided (see STL 224).

What Should We Sing during the *Rites of Ordination*?

The *General Introduction to the Rites of Ordination* makes two points with regard to the celebration of the Sacrament and liturgical music:

> Ordination is to be celebrated with the rites of Mass, in which the faithful, particularly on a Sunday, take an active part "at one altar at which the Bishop presides, surrounded by his presbyterate and ministers." In this way the preeminent manifestation of the Church and the conferral of Holy Orders are joined with the eucharistic Sacrifice, the fount and apex of the whole Christian life. (RO 9)
>
> It belongs to the Conferences of Bishops to adapt the rites of Ordination of a Bishop, of priests, and of deacons to the needs of the particular regions, so that, after the Apostolic See has confirmed the decisions of a Conference, the rites may be used in the region of that Conference. With due regard for local circumstances and conditions,

---

54. See SC, no. 61; CCC, no. 1621. [Footnote in STL]

55. See RM, no. 30; SC, nos. 118, 121. [Footnote in STL]

and for the genius and traditions of the various peoples, the Conferences of Bishops have the authority: . . . e) to approve certain liturgical songs to be used instead of those given in this book . . . . (RO 11)

Notes and Comments.   The celebration of the Sacrament of Holy Orders signifies a unique manifestation of the Church and this sign dimension of the Sacrament is enhanced as it occurs with the Bishop celebrant with his priests and sacred ministers and the faithful participating in the course of the Sunday Eucharist. Such a solemn expression of the Church and, consequently, of her faith, especially in the mystery of the Sacrament of Holy Orders requires authentic and carefully chosen liturgical music. What has already been said about singing the Eucharist above applies here for this celebration of Holy Orders. Since such a celebration of the Eucharist with the rites of Holy Orders belongs to one of the Church's fullest self-expressions, even new ritual music should be approved as an adaptation by the Conference of Bishops.

    The Entrance and Communion chants correspond to the Mass chosen for the celebration of the Sacrament (see STL 225). Whether the Mass occurs on a Sunday or solemnity or if it is the ritual Mass "For the Conferral of Holy Orders," the outline of options for these chants in the *General Instruction of the Roman Missal* applies. The recited antiphons in the *Roman Missal* for the Mass to be celebrated can serve as a possible textual source to guide the choice of a suitable liturgical song.

    At times during the rites of Ordination for a Bishop, a priest and a deacon, there is the acclamation, "Thanks be to God," on the part of the people. Another suitable acclamation may replace, "Thanks be to God," which captures its import.[56]

    With the Ordination of a Bishop, which begins after the proclamation of the Gospel, all stand and sing the hymn, *Veni, Creator Spiritus.* If custom dictates the use of something other than *Veni, Creator Spiritus,* it is to be similar to it. Since the use of the hymn, *Veni, Creator Spiritus,* belongs in a unique way to the Ordination of a Bishop, it should ordinarily not find a place in the Ordination of priests and deacons.[57]

---

56. See 38, 74, 122, 150, 198, 226, 264, 305.
57. See 35, 71.

In each of the three rites of Ordination for the Bishop, priests, and deacons, the Litany of Supplication takes place (see STL 226). This litany is sung as given in the ritual book with respect for the form in each of the rites which differs with the order. The litany for the ordination of a Bishop includes all of the Apostles and Bishop saints. The litany for the ordination of priests includes presbyter saints while the litany for the ordination of deacons includes deacon saints. Again, as with the litany at the Easter Vigil, it is always possible to add additional canonized saints to the litanies according to the directives in the ritual book while introducing the additions in the proper place according to category and chronology.[58]

The essential elements of the ordination are the laying on of hands and the prayer of ordination. The laying on of hands takes place in silence on the part of all.[59] The musical notation is provided for each of the three prayers of ordination, Bishop, priest, and deacon.[60] The norm, as with the principal prayer of other sacramental celebrations, is for the Bishop celebrant to sing the prayer of ordination. Singing gives solemn expression to the faith of the Church announced in these prayers. The faithful sing, "Amen," to these prayers in the same manner in which they respond to the Eucharistic Prayer. The "Amen" is a response and not an independent rite apart from the prayer that an elaborate musical setting might suggest.

In each of the three rites of Ordination there is very little that is sung during the explanatory rites. Typically, an antiphon and psalm are proposed when there is no spoken liturgical formula for a particular part of the rite. With the ordination of a Bishop during the fraternal kiss, Psalm 95 with the appointed antiphon is sung. An appropriate liturgical song may be used if similar in theme, especially if Psalm 95 served as the Responsorial Psalm of the Mass.[61] With the ordination of priests during the investiture with stole and chasuble and the anointing of hands, Psalm 109 with the appointed antiphon is sung. An appropriate liturgical song may be used if similar in theme, especially if Psalm 109 served as the Responsorial

---

58. See RO 42, 98, 127, 155, 203, 231, 273, 314.

59. See RO 45, 81, 130, 158, 206, 234, 276, 284, 317, 325.

60. See RO 47, 131, 207.

61. See RO 57, 93.

Psalm of the Mass (see STL 226).[62] The rite of Ordination for priests provides a choice between a responsory with musical notation or Psalm 99 with the appointed antiphon to accompany the fraternal kiss. Likewise, an appropriate liturgical song may be used if similar in theme, especially if Psalm 99 served as the Responsorial Psalm of the Mass (see STL 226).[63] With the ordination of deacons during the investiture with the stole and dalmatic and the handing on of the *Book of Gospels*, Psalm 83 with the appointed antiphon is sung. An appropriate liturgical song may be used if similar in theme, especially if Psalm 83 served as the Responsorial Psalm of the Mass (see STL 226).[64] During the fraternal kiss Psalm 145 with the appointed antiphon is sung. Another suitable liturgical song may replace Psalm 145 if similar in theme (see STL 226).[65]

During the ordination of a Bishop after the Prayer after Communion, the hymn *Te Deum* is sung. If custom dictates the use of something other than *Te Deum*, it should be similar to it.[66]

Conclusion

The rites for all the Sacraments provide ample occasions to sing during the course of their celebration. Singing the sacraments allows all those participating to engage more deeply the Mysteries being celebrated so to grasp more fully the saving deeds of the Lord at work here and now. Therefore, the important choice to sing also includes what to sing which arises from the texts and examples in the rites. This makes all the more apparent the need for composers to be attentive to what is indicated in the rites for what we should sing, with a faithful adherence to the texts. Composers are encouraged to provide such compositions as a most formative and valuable way to assist pastors, music ministers and the whole liturgical assembly to sing the Mysteries of the Sacraments (see STL 200).

All of the Sacraments include a celebration of the Liturgy of the Word, which draws attention to the announcement of the saving

---

62. See RO 134, 162, 288, 329.
63. See RO 137, 165, 291, 332.
64. See RO 209, 237, 279, 320.
65. See RO 212, 240.
66. See RO 61, 97.

work of the Lord to be realized in the Sacrament. As pastors and music ministers, we need to prepare for the sung Liturgy of the Word, as we do during Mass, to highlight this fundamental connection between the Word of God and the Sacraments. Also, all of the Sacraments, except for the Sacrament of Penance and Reconciliation, can be or should be celebrated within Mass. When this occurs, in addition to what we should sing during the celebration of the Sacrament, the principles outlined above for singing the Eucharist should also be in place.

You may be surprised by the lack of specific examples of what to sing when what the rite provides cannot be sung or when you choose the option to sing an "appropriate" or "suitable" liturgical song. This lack is deliberate since the suggestion of such songs would be unnecessarily restrictive and fail to encourage the actual singing of the ritual texts. As pastors and music ministers, we encourage you to make this choice, keeping in mind all of the possibilities and the rich significance of what is already provided. Choose to sing the Sacraments with the first possibility being the indicated texts and then, with the judgments in mind and a proper understanding of what is "appropriate" or "suitable," consider an alternative when pastorally necessary. Most of all, sing the Sacraments!

Chapter 8

How Do We Sing the Liturgy of the Hours?

INTRODUCTION

The Liturgy of the Hours celebrates the same Mystery of Christ, the Mystery of Christ's death and Resurrection, as the Eucharist and all of the Sacraments. Thus, like liturgical singing during the Eucharist and the other Sacraments, so liturgical singing during the Divine Office is worship of this divine Mystery. This celebration of the Sacred Liturgy, the Liturgy of the Hours, like the Eucharist and all the Sacraments, belongs to the whole Church (see GILOH 20–27).

Pastors and liturgical music ministers need to carefully review the *General Instruction of the Liturgy of the Hours* to deepen an understanding of this celebration of the Sacred Liturgy. A good place to begin is to examine GI OH 23 and SC 100. An important dimension of this understanding is the essential role of singing the Liturgy of the Hours. The *General Instruction of the Liturgy of the Hours* provides detailed directives on singing the different elements in the Divine Office, especially the psalms, as well as how to carry out a sung celebration of an Hour.

SINGING THE PSALMODY

Chapter 3 of the *General Instruction of the Liturgy of the Hours* addresses the various ways of singing the psalms. It is helpful at this point to present completely what this instruction says about singing the psalms which *Sing to the Lord* summarily indicates.

Different psalms may be sung in different ways for a fuller grasp of their spiritual meaning and beauty. The choice of ways is dictated by the literary genre or length of each psalm, by the language used, whether Latin or the vernacular, and especially by the kind of celebration, whether individual, with a group, or with a congregation. The reason for using psalms is not the establishment of a fixed amount of prayer but their own variety and the character proper to each.

The psalms are sung or said in one of three ways, according to the different usages established in tradition or experience: directly (in directum), that is, all sing the entire psalm, or antiphonally, that is, two choirs or sections of the congregation sing alternate verses or strophes, or responsorially.

At the beginning of each psalm its own antiphon is always to be recited, as noted in nos. 113–120. At the end of the psalm the practice of concluding with the Glory to the Father and As it was in the beginning is retained. This is the fitting conclusion endorsed by tradition and it gives to Old Testament prayer a note of praise and a Christological and Trinitarian sense. The antiphon may be repeated at the end of the psalm.

When longer psalms occur, sections are marked in the psalter that divides the parts in such a way as to keep the threefold structure of the hour; but great care has been taken not to distort the meaning of the psalm.

It is useful to observe this division, especially in a choral celebration in Latin; the Glory to the Father is added at the end of each section.

It is permissible, however, either to keep this traditional way or to pause between the different sections of the same psalm or to recite the whole psalm and its antiphon as a single unit without a break.

In addition, when the literary genre of a psalm suggests it, the divisions into strophes are marked in order that, especially when the psalm is sung in the vernacular, the antiphons may be repeated after each strophe; in this case the Glory to the Father need be said only at the end of the psalm. (GILOH 121–125)

Notes and Comments.   All parts of the Liturgy of the Hours, including the readings, can be sung, and in its most solemn form should be sung. The psalms above all should be sung (see STL 232). Singing the psalms allows for "a fuller grasp of their spiritual meaning and beauty." The above directives, clearly and purposely expressed, from the instruction for the Liturgy of Hours serves us well when preparing for the sung celebration of the Office.

Sing to the Lord repeats these directives about the psalms somewhat when it states that the psalms may be sung in a responsorial,

antiphonal, or through-composed form (see STL 233–235). The choice
for the form, as indicated by the instruction above, depends on the
psalm itself, and then on the language used and those singing the
psalms. Careful attention should be given to singing the proper antiphons because of their interpretive relationship to the psalms. The
division of the psalms should be respected within an Hour when the
psalm is sung.

Sing to the Lord suggests the use of metrical psalms in the
celebration of the Liturgy of the Hours (see STL 236). The benefit of
this suggestion is to promote the actual singing of texts derived from
the word of God for the Liturgy of the Hours. However, the use of
a strophic hymn, most likely with a familiar hymn melody, and even
if the metrical text is rather faithful to the original psalm, is not in
complete agreement with the form and tradition of the sung psalmody
in the Liturgy of the Hours. It must be remembered that in Christian
prayer the form for singing the psalms originates in the Jewish
prayer. Our contemporary manner for singing the psalms should carry
and continue their original Jewish form. This is a point to consider
when evaluating the suggestion in *Sing to the Lord* to introduce a psalm
in metric form in accord with more recent Protestant and Catholic
practice in celebrations of the Liturgy of the Hours (see STL 236).
The place for a strophic hymn in the Office is the hymn itself which
will be discussed below.

The sung psalmody, in addition to the three traditional forms,
allows for the psalms to be accompanied or not, and if accompanied,
then by various instruments. Likewise, the psalms can be sung by all,
or by a few, or by one member of the liturgical assembly, or a choir
(see STL 239).

Sing to the Lord advises other formula tones for vernacular
singing of the psalmody rather than Gregorian tones which are better
suited for Latin singing (see STL 237–238). Recent magisterial
instruction has been clear that when new tones are devised for vernacular singing they are to be inspired by the tradition as a way to
translate the tradition into the new idiom.[1] The inspiration of the
traditional tone, for example singing the psalms with Gregorian tones,

---

1. Chirograph, 12.

highlights how the tone supports and carries the text and does not obscure or diminish the text.[2]

Singing the Hymn

The hymn in the *Liturgy of the Hours* requires some careful attention. Chapter 3 of the *General Instruction of the Liturgy of the Hours* addresses the singing of the hymn and other non-biblical songs. It is helpful to note all of what GILOH says about singing the hymn.

> A very ancient tradition gives hymns the place in the office that they still retain. By their mystical and poetic character they are specifically designed for God's praise. But they also are an element for the people; in fact more often than the other parts of the office the hymns bring out the proper theme of individual hours or feasts and incline and draw the spirit to a devout celebration. The beauty of their language often adds to this power. Furthermore, in the office hymns are the main poetic element created by the Church.
>
> A hymn follows the traditional rule of ending with a doxology, usually addressed to the same divine person as the hymn itself.
>
> In the office for Ordinary Time, to ensure variety, a twofold cycle of hymns is given for each hour, for use in alternate weeks.
>
> In addition, a twofold cycle of hymns has been introduced into the office of readings for Ordinary Time, one for use at night and the other for use during the day.
>
> New hymns can be set to traditional melodies of the same rhythm and meter.
>
> For vernacular celebration, the conferences of bishops may adapt the Latin hymns to suit the character of their own language and introduce fresh compositions, provided these are in complete harmony with the spirit of the hour, season, or feast. Great care must be taken not to allow popular songs that have no artistic merit and are not in keeping with the dignity of the liturgy. (GILOH 173–178)

Notes and Comments.   The Office hymn is one of the more misunderstood elements of the Liturgy of the Hours. Some insist that the

---

2. An excellent available resource which builds upon this point is *The Mundelein Psalter.* The Mundelein Psalter is the first complete one-volume edition containing the approved English-language texts of the Liturgy of the Hours with psalms that are pointed for the chanting of the Divine Office. The music consists of simple yet beautiful Gregorian-based modes composed for this Psalter. (See Douglas Martis, ed., *The Mundelein Psalter* (Chicago, Mundelein, IL: Hillenbrand Books, 2007)

hymn at the beginning of the Hour serves the celebration in a similar way as the Entrance at Mass. Others consider the hymn an optional element of the Liturgy of the Hours, even in public celebrations. *The hymn is an obligatory element of each Hour of the Office.* It serves a unique purpose within the Hour. This poetic element crafted by the Church with a centuries old tradition gives shape to the particular Hour in the way the hymn identifies the time of the day, the liturgical season, or the liturgical observance. In the typical edition of the Liturgy of the Hours some hymns are proper to a particular Office. The hymn, in keeping with the whole liturgical orientation of the Liturgy of the Hours, typically concludes with a doxology. This doxology informs those singing the hymn that this humanly composed part of the Liturgy of the Hours, as with the whole of the Hour, leads us to the worship of God.

Sing to the Lord only says that the hymn is to be sung (see STL 240). We need to elaborate slightly more on the choice of the Office hymn since, in many cases, its role and nature are so misunderstood. Also, a tendency to choose popular hymns which may indeed offend the dignity of the Liturgy must also be countered today as indicated in the instruction above. When choices are made for the hymn, in addition to keeping in mind the time of the day, the liturgical season, and the liturgical observance, the hymn in the typical edition should inspire the choice. The hymns given in the typical edition serve as the best examples how a hymn can tell the time of the day, the season, and observance for a particular hour of the Office. Finally, a paraphrase of a psalm should not be sung in place of the hymn since the psalms have their own unique purpose as the principle element in the Liturgy of the Hours.

Singing an Hour of the Office

Every part of an hour of the Divine Office may be sung. Chapter 5 of the *General Instruction for the Liturgy of the Hours* provides a complete description of the rubrics and norms on how to do just this (GILOH 267–284). It is helpful to review with special attention this chapter of General Instruction of the Liturgy of the Hours when preparing the singing of an hour of the Office.

Sing to the Lord does not reference this important section of the instruction for the Liturgy of the Hours except with a cursory mention of sung elements (see STL 240). The principle of progressive solemnity, which is described in Chapter 4 of this book, finds its modern origin in this section of the *General Instruction of the Liturgy of the Hours* (see GILOH 273).

In the instruction, the point is reinforced that the singing of the Office is the norm for the Roman Rite and that every effort should be made so that such a norm typify the communal celebration. Singing the Office, as with any sung celebration of the Sacred Liturgy, manifests the faith of the liturgical assembly in the divine event that is unfolding and thus its solemn sung expression. Sunday and solemnities are days above all when sung celebrations should take place and especially with the principal Hours of Morning Prayer and Evening Prayer.

Latin, and other vernacular languages, may be used, as with all liturgical celebrations, to enhance the possibilities of a sung celebration. Following the principles of progressive solemnity, the psalms above all are to be sung along with the canticles and their respective antiphons. Other parts, because of their nature, call for singing, for example, the acclamations, the dialogues, the responses, and intercessions. The Gospel canticles in Morning and Evening Prayer are like the Gospel during the celebration of the Eucharist where the Lord himself is speaking. However, unlike during the Eucharist, it is the liturgical assembly that sings the Gospel canticle and in so doing is reminded of its dignity and content. The Lord's Prayer, which occurs during Morning and Evening Prayer, uniquely links these two Hours to the celebration of the Eucharist and for that reason suggests that it be sung.

In many of our communities, singing the Liturgy of the Hours continues to be an exception, even on Sundays and during the privileged seasons of the Church Year. One of the more successful ways to introduce singing the Liturgy of the Hours is to begin gradually and with some catechesis on this particular celebration of the Sacred Liturgy. Also, the patterns for progressive solemnity applied to the celebration of the Eucharist should typically be mirrored in the celebration of the Liturgy of the Hours.

CONCLUSION

The Liturgy of the Hours continues throughout the day the saving Sacrifice of the Lord celebrated in the Eucharist. Singing the Liturgy of the Hours, as with singing the Eucharist and the other Sacraments, gives fitting expression to the Church's voice in praise of the Father in the Mystery of Christ. Pastors and liturgical music ministers should make every effort to provide for occasions, especially on Sundays, when the faithful can assemble for sung celebrations of the Hours (see STL 231).[3] The next chapter looks at singing other liturgical rites.

---

3. See SC 100, GILOH 23.

Chapter 9

How Do We Sing Other Liturgical Rites?

INTRODUCTION

Throughout this book we have consistently discussed the emphasis the Church places on singing the actual texts and rites of the Sacred Liturgy. Singing is part of the Christian voice for the expression, communication, and manifestation of the Christian Faith. When singing the Eucharist and the other Sacraments is normative then it forms the liturgical assembly to sing during other liturgical rites. All of the same theological and liturgical points already discussed in this book; such as why we sing, the regard for the roles and duties of those ordained and liturgical music ministers, how we choose liturgical music, and observing patterns of progressive solemnity, guide the planning and actual celebration of other liturgical rites. Pastors and liturgical music ministers need to keep in mind that the liturgical assembly for these rites gather with very different needs and expectations than the Sunday assembly, especially when gathering for funerals and blessings. Carefully chosen and prepared liturgical music will properly orient those assembled, having a wide variety of emotions and sentiments, for divine worship.

In this final chapter, we discuss what we should sing in the *Sunday Celebrations in the Absence of a Priest*, in celebrations of *Holy Communion and the Worship of the Eucharist Outside Mass*, in the *Order of Christian Funerals*, and in the *Book of Blessings*. As in the chapters about what we should sing during the Eucharist and the other Sacraments, this chapter will focus on the texts given in each of the ritual books for singing. Also, in this chapter, you will see that there are several occasions when an "appropriate" or "suitable" song may be chosen instead of what is provided in the liturgical book. While we do not give specific examples of alternative songs, again your choice for an "appropriate" or "suitable" song is measured by the ritual occasion, the example of proposed texts, both what the text says and the nature of the text, and the musical capacity of those singing.

What Should We Sing During the *Sunday Celebrations in the Absence of a Priest?*

In *Sing to the Lord*, the Bishops properly reiterate that the rites for Sunday celebrations in the absence of a priest are obviously intended for exceptional circumstances. As such, these rites include possible celebrations of Morning or Evening Prayer of the Liturgy of the Hours or a Liturgy of the Word. Both types of celebration may include the distribution of Holy Communion (see STL 241). What has already been stated above about liturgical music with the celebration of the Liturgy of the Hours itself and the Liturgy of the Word during Mass should be observed in the use of this ritual book. The Bishops are clear with their encouragement of singing in Sunday celebrations in the absence of a priest (see STL 241).

When Holy Communion is distributed, the communion procession is accompanied by an appropriate psalm or suitable liturgical song. The choice for liturgical music for the Communion procession could be the same as for the Mass of the Sunday.

The ritual book for Sunday celebrations in the absence of a priest calls for an Act of Thanksgiving in celebrations of the Liturgy of the Word. Specifically, according to the ritual book this Act of Thanksgiving includes possible sung psalms, hymns, or canticles.[1]

The absence of the priest is a sacramental loss in the celebration of the Lord's Day. However, the liturgical music ministers as well as the whole liturgical assembly are in no way diminished in their duties and responsibilities to contribute as they do at Sunday Mass to the celebration of the Mystery of Christ in the Liturgy of the Hours or a Liturgy of the Word with liturgical music that gives glory to God and helps all assembled to grow in holiness.

---

1. See SCAP 44.

What Should We Sing During Celebrations of *Holy Communion and the Worship of the Eucharist outside Mass?*

The ritual book *Holy Communion and the Worship of the Eucharist outside Mass* contains a variety of rites for the distribution of Holy Communion and the worship of the Blessed Sacrament outside of the celebration of Mass. *Sing to the Lord* importantly notes that the adoration of the exposed Blessed Sacrament is a liturgical action (see STL 242). Therefore, these rites, as outlined in *Holy Communion and the Worship of the Eucharist outside Mass*, are to be observed with the same attentiveness and fidelity as those described in other liturgical books. However, there is a great deal of flexibility when it comes to choosing liturgical music for these rites, always keeping in mind what has already been established in Chapter 3 for making these choices.

The Bishops do not address the frequent use of the first chapter of this ritual book, which describes the distribution of Holy Communion outside of Mass with the celebration of the Word.[2] This frequently used rite pertains to the circumstances when Mass is not celebrated. Nonetheless, what is described for liturgical music during the Liturgy of the Word, the distribution of Holy Communion, and the period after Communion during Mass as previously described applies to this celebration as well.

Chapter 3 of the ritual book describes three forms of worship of the Holy Eucharist with the first form being the more common of the three. This first form is the rite of Eucharistic exposition and benediction. Song is an integral aspect of the worship of the Eucharist with this rite. After all assemble for the rite, a song may be sung as the minister approaches the altar for exposition (see STL 243).[3] During the period of exposition and adoration, in addition to the prayers and readings, there may also be songs to direct the attention of those in adoration to the worship of the Lord (see STL 243).[4] Toward the end of the exposition and during the incensation of the Blessed Sacrament a hymn is sung (see STL 243).[5] The U.S. Bishops

---

2. See HCWEM 26–53.

3. See HCWEM 93.

4. See HCWEM 95.

5. See HCWEM 97.

rightfully suggest that this hymn be "particularly appropriate for the adoration of the Blessed Sacrament, rather than those more suited to accompany the procession to receive Holy Communion at Mass."[6] During the reposition of the Blessed Sacrament, that is after the blessing, an acclamation may be sung (see STL 243).

What has already been stated above concerning liturgical music during the Liturgy of the Word and the Collect applies to this celebration of the word and the prayer before the Blessed Sacrament.

Pastors and liturgical music ministers have an opportunity with celebrations of exposition and benediction of the Most Blessed Sacrament to plan occasions rich in faith and devotion by the choices for music that will help the faithful to associate this rite with the celebration of Mass (see STL 242).[7] Eucharistic exposition and benediction also provides an opportunity for the use of music from the tradition, such as the Latin hymns that are often associated with this Eucharistic devotion.

WHAT SHOULD WE SING DURING THE *ORDER OF CHRISTIAN FUNERALS?*

The *General Introduction to the Order of Christian Funerals* states the significance of liturgical music in all of the funeral rites, the role music it has in the comfort and consolation of the family and mourners, and its purpose, which is to give emphasis to the paschal mystery celebrated in the funeral of a Christian. Let's briefly examine what the *Order of Christian Funerals* states

> Music is integral to the funeral rites. It allows the community to express convictions and feelings that words alone may fail to convey. It has the power to console and uplift mourners and to strengthen the unity of the assembly in faith and love. The texts of songs chosen for a particular celebration should express the paschal mystery of the Lord's suffering, death, and triumph over death and should be related to the readings from Scripture.
>
> Since music can evoke strong feelings, the music for the celebration of the funeral rites should be chosen with great care. The music at funerals should support, console, and uplift the participants and should help to

---

6. STL 243.
7. See HCWEM 82.

create in them a spirit of hope in Christ's victory over death and in the Christian's share in that victory.

Music should be provided for the vigil and funeral liturgy and, whenever possible, for the funeral processions and the rite of committal. The specific notes that precede each of these rites suggest places in the rites where music is appropriate. Many musical settings used by the parish community during the liturgical year may be suitable for use at funerals. Efforts should be made to develop and expand the parish's repertoire for use at funerals.

An organist or other instrumentalist, a cantor, and whenever possible, even a choir should assist the assembly's full participation in singing the songs, responses, and acclamations of these rites. (OCF 30–33)

Liturgical music during the celebration of the funeral rites assumes many different roles, perhaps more so than in other liturgical rites. The music is at once expressive of the Christian Faith in the Paschal Mystery of Christ celebrated in funeral rites, expressive of the faith and prayers of those celebrating, especially the mourners, and a source of consolation and hope. As pastors and liturgical music ministers, planning must be with care and consideration of not only the liturgical dimensions of choices but also of the unique role of music during the funeral rites. Since music plays such an exceptional role in the *Order of Christian Funerals*, then it should be a part of all of the funeral rites (see STL 246–247). In order to meet this expectation of the *Order of Christian Funerals*, we need to be committed to providing the necessary liturgical music ministers for all of the rites.

Singing the funeral rites, as with singing all of the Church's rites, sings the praise of God. This orientation of liturgical music in the celebration of a funeral is safeguarded when the choice for music is not to memorialize the deceased but rather for divine worship (see STL 248). *Sing to the Lord* correctly includes "[s]ecular music, even though it may reflect on the background, character, interests, or personal preferences of the deceased or mourners, it is not appropriate for the Sacred Liturgy" (STL 246).

What Should We Sing during the *Vigil for the Deceased?*

Music is integral to any vigil, especially the vigil for the deceased. In the difficult circumstances following death, well-chosen music can touch the mourners and others present at levels of human need that words alone often fail to reach. Such music can enliven the faith of the community gathered to support the family and to affirm hope in the resurrection.

Whenever possible, an instrumentalist and a cantor or leader of song should assist the assembly's full participation in the singing.

In the choice of music for the vigil, preference should be given to the singing of the opening song and the responsorial psalm. The litany, the Lord's Prayer, and a closing song may also be sung. (OCF 68)

The Office for the Dead taken from the Liturgy of the Hours may also serve as the principal rite during the time following death and before the Funeral Liturgy.[8] When the Liturgy of the Hours is celebrated as part of the Christian funeral, again all that has been previously described about the selection of liturgical music for the Office applies with special attention to the unique role of music and funerals.

Notes and Comments.   The Vigil for the Deceased can take two forms, at a station apart from the church or with the reception of the body at the church. The *Order of Christian Funerals* is clear about the role of liturgical music during the vigil and states a preference for what should be sung. It is too easy to set aside singing during the Vigil in favor of reciting all of its parts. In addition to the music during the Vigil serving to "touch the mourners and others present at levels of human need that words alone often fail to reach," this use of liturgical music, as in every celebration of the Liturgy, gives expression to what the Church believes. The Opening Song in the vigil is not described. It seems obvious that this song may be an appropriate psalm or hymn for the occasion or even to the liturgical season when the Vigil takes place. The Responsorial Psalm can be sung in one of the several ways identified in the *General Instruction of the Roman Missal*. In addition to singing the litany, the Lord's Prayer, and a closing song, the dialogues and blessing may also be sung (see STL 250). The Vigil for the Deceased with Reception at the Church includes an entrance procession accompanied by a psalm, song, or responsory (see STL 249).[9] *Sing to the Lord* echoes the rite when it calls for silence or song to conclude the Vigil for the Deceased

---

8. See OCF 54, Part IV.
9. See OCF 85.

(see STL 249–250). In fact, the rite actually suggests the possibility of both song and silence to conclude the vigil.[10]

What Should We Sing During the Funeral Liturgy?

In the directions and description of the Funeral Liturgy much is mentioned with regard to liturgical music and musicians. The parts highlighted below provide indications what should be sung, with some examples during the course of the Funeral Liturgy. The Funeral Liturgy can be celebrated both with Mass and outside of Mass. Of course, what has already been described about singing the Eucharist applies to the Funeral Mass as well. Let's examine what the *Order of Christian Funerals* says:

> To draw the community together in prayer at the beginning of the funeral liturgy, the procession should be accompanied, whenever possible, by the singing of the entrance song. This song ought to be a profound expression of belief in eternal life and the resurrection of the dead as well as prayer of intercession for the deceased. (See, for example, OCF 403).[11]
>
> The responsorial psalm enables the community to respond in faith to the first reading. Through the psalms the community expresses its grief and praise, and acknowledges its Creator and Redeemer as the sure source of trust and hope in times of trial. Since the responsorial psalm is a song, whenever possible, it should be sung. Psalms may be sung responsorially, with the response sung by the assembly and all the verses by the cantor or choir, or directly, with no response and all the verses sung by all or by the cantor or choir. When not sung, the responsorial psalm after the reading should be recited in a manner conducive to mediation on the word of God. (OCF, 139)
>
> The liturgy of the Eucharist takes place in the usual manner at the funeral Mass. Members of the family or friends of the deceased should bring the gifts to the altar. Instrumental music or song (for example, Psalm 18, Psalm 63, Psalm 66:13–20, or Psalm 138) may accompany the procession with the gifts. . . . Since music gives greater solemnity to a ritual action, the singing of the people's parts of the eucharistic prayer should be encouraged, that is, the responses to the preface dialogue, the Sanctus, the memorial acclamation, and the Great Amen. To reinforce and to express

---

10. See OCF 81, 97.

11. OCF 135. The OLF, 403, provides samples of songs and hymns that are suitable for the entrance song of the Funeral Liturgy.

more fully the unity of the congregation during the communion rite, the people may sing the Lord's Prayer, the doxology, the Lamb of God, and a song for the communion procession (for example, Psalm 23, Psalm 27, Psalm 34, Psalm 63, or Psalm 121). (OCF 144, in part)

The song of farewell, which should affirm hope and trust in the paschal mystery, is the climax of the rite of final commendation. It should be sung to a melody simple enough for all to sing. It may take the form of a responsory or even a hymn. When singing it is not possible, invocations may be recited by the assembly. (OCF 147, in part)

Especially when accompanied with music and singing, the procession can help to reinforce the bond of communion between the participants. Whenever possible, psalms or songs may accompany the entire procession from the church to the place of committal. In situations where a solemn procession on foot from the Church to the place of committal is not possible, an antiphon or song may be sung as the body is being taken to the entrance of the church. Psalms, hymns or liturgical songs may also be sung by the participants as they gather at the place of committal. (OLF 149)

An organist or other instrumentalist, a cantor, and whenever possible, a choir should be present to assist the congregation in singing the songs, responses, and acclamations of the funeral liturgy. (OCF 153)

The *Order of Christian Funeral* with its introduction to each of the forms for the Funeral Liturgy also highlights what should be sung specifically for the Funeral Mass and for the Funeral outside Mass. For the Funeral Mass:

In the choice of music for the funeral Mass, preference should be given to the singing of the acclamations, the responsorial psalm, the entrance and communion songs, and especially the song of farewell at the final commendation. (OCF 157)

For the Funeral Liturgy Outside Mass:

In the choice of music for the funeral liturgy, preference should be given to the singing of the entrance song, the responsorial psalm, the gospel acclamation, and especially the song of farewell as the final commendation. (OCF 181)

Notes and Comments.   The ritual book as noted above lists preferences for what should be sung during a Funeral Liturgy, both with a Funeral Mass and a Funeral Liturgy outside of Mass. In both cases, the parts to be sung should be typical of a sung celebration of the Sacred Liturgy.

The liturgical musical choices for the entrance and communion processions should consider the listing in the *General Instruction of the Roman Missal*. The antiphons given in the Masses for the Dead in the *Roman Missal* serve as an excellent source to inspire a choice for other psalmody and antiphons or another suitable liturgical song (see STL 252).

The *Order of Christian Funerals* gives examples of both Songs of Farewell, as well as for the procession to the place of committal (see STL 253–254). These are two different accompanying chants for two different ritual actions. If these given choices for either ritual actions are set aside, then what is chosen should relate in theme and purpose to the given examples for the respective chants. Especially at these parts of the Funeral Liturgy, secular music, even if it promotes Christian sentiment with regard to death, is out of place.

Part V of the Order of Christian Funerals, Additional Texts, provides a variety of texts which may substitute for the same type provided with the rites.

Singing the Funeral Liturgy should be the norm with a well-suited repertoire for the Funeral Liturgy and the Paschal victory it celebrates. Music from the Liturgical Year also has a place in the Funeral Liturgy which, when appropriate, links the mourners with a participation in the overall observance of the Church in the Mysteries of Christ.

What Should We Sing During the *Rite of Committal?*

What the Order of Christian Funerals *says:*

> The singing of well chosen music at the rite of committal can help the mourners as they face the reality of separation. At the rite of committal with final commendation, whenever possible, the song of farewell should be sung. In either form of the committal rite, a hymn or liturgical song that affirms hope in God's mercy and in the resurrection of the dead is desirable at the conclusion of the rite. (OCF 214)

Notes and Comments. Music should accompany the Rite of Committal (see STL 247). In addition to the Song of Farewell, if it is part of the rite of committal, and a song at its conclusion, the prayers over the place of committal and the committal itself could be sung along with the intercessions, the Lord's Prayer, the concluding prayer, and the conclusion to the rite (see STL 256).

All throughout the funeral rites, an emphasis is given to the singing of the psalms, the hymnody of the Christian, as a traditional way to celebrate the Mystery of Christ and as words of consolation to the mourners, and to accompany the processions and rites of the funeral (see STL 244–245, 251, 255).[12] The *Order of Christian Funerals* identifies Psalms 25, 93, 116, 118, 119, 122 with given antiphons for these processions.[13] Pastors and liturgical music ministers, with the help of catechesis, might gradually introduce the singing of the psalms once again in the course of the funeral rites, especially for the processions to the church and the place of burial (see STL 247).[14]

Once again, in order to meet this expectation of the *Order of Christian Funerals* for liturgical music at funerals, we need to be committed to providing the necessary liturgical music ministers for the Funeral Liturgy. *Sing to the Lord* includes the fine suggestion of promoting the practice of funeral choirs to do just this (see STL 257).

WHAT SHOULD WE SING IN THE *BOOK OF BLESSINGS?*

The *Book of Blessings* is not discussed in *Sing to the Lord*. The *General Introduction to the Book of Blessings* does not specifically address liturgical music in the celebration of Blessings. As a liturgical book, however, it often indicates, especially as part of the Introductory Rites and Concluding Rite of a particular blessing, that a suitable song open and close the celebration. In the section, Celebration of a Blessing, the typical structure is described with specific mention of an intervening psalm or song between the readings.[15] In planning the celebration, a cantor or psalmist and choir should fulfill their proper function.[16] In the course of certain Blessings when the celebrant sprinkles those

---

12. See OCF 42.
13. See OCF 127, 176, 203.
14. See OCF 42, 149.
15. See BB 21.
16. See BB 24a.

present or a place or an object with holy water, a suitable song is sung. The Lord's Prayer, when prescribed, may also be sung.

Several Blessings can be carried out within Mass. When a Blessing is carried out in this way, what has already been described about liturgical music and the Mass should, of course, be considered.

Notes and Comments.   The *Book of Blessings*, as the circumstances of its use suggest, allows for a great deal of legitimate flexibility guided by the directives in its general introduction. However, with this possible flexibility, the fact that these Blessings are liturgical celebrations and, as such, celebrations with all of the dimensions of a liturgical celebration, music and song deserve primary consideration. As with all celebrations of the Sacred Liturgy the dialogues between the celebrant and the faithful should be sung as they are at Mass. The principle prayer or blessing within the rite should also be chanted with the sung "Amen" of the faithful. During the course of the Reading of the Word of God what would be typically sung during the course of the Liturgy of the Word could also be sung on the occasion of a Blessing, especially the psalm. The Reading of the Word of God can vary in its structure from a single Gospel reading to a full Liturgy of the Word as on Sunday.

The choice for music should take into consideration the liturgical occasion or season as well as the intended purpose and topic of the Blessing. Likewise, the principles of progressive solemnity should be applied. Some blessings are considered more solemn than others with the Bishop as celebrant.

What Should We Sing during Popular Devotions?

In *Sing to the Lord*, the Bishops rightfully highlight the role of music in popular devotions (see STL 258). Devotions offer a wide range of occasions for singing popular religious music both from the tradition and newly composed which is not suited to the celebration of the Sacred Liturgy.[17] Although the choice of this music may be made without the boundaries of the rites and texts found in the liturgical books, it should, however, be subject to the judgments for music described above. The *Directory on Popular Piety and the Liturgy:*

---

17. See DPPL 17.

Principles and Guidelines, by the Congregation for Divine Worship and the Discipline of the Sacraments, is a helpful resource for planning devotions and the use of music. Certainly, when elements of the Sacred Liturgy are included in popular devotions what is described above for singing these elements should be observed.

CONCLUSION

Singing other liturgical rites allows for the theological and liturgical guides to singing the Eucharist, the other Sacraments, and the Liturgy of the Hours, to underscore the planning and celebration of every dimension of the Church at prayer. Singing other liturgical rites with the encouragement of pastors and liturgical music ministers fosters a deepening appreciation of the role of singing whenever the Church assembles to worship God and that music in the celebration of the Liturgy is a part of divine worship.

This third and most substantial part of this book develops the theological and liturgical points identified by *Sing to the Lord* when it answers the important questions of why we sing the Liturgy, what are the responsibilities of the ordained and faithful, especially liturgical music ministers, how to choose music for the liturgy, and what are the patterns for singing the liturgy. It is all of these questions and answers reviewed in Parts I and II of this book that surround the imperative that we sing the Eucharist, the other Sacraments, the liturgy of the Hours, and other liturgical rites. Sing the liturgy! Singing the liturgy is an expectation grounded in and governed by the liturgical books. Singing the liturgy gives new and necessary appreciation for the actual texts indicated for song in these books. We should not fear the challenge of singing the liturgy even with our various circumstances and resources. Instead, as pastors and liturgical music ministers, we should see this challenge as a grace-filled opportunity to assist others to sing to the Lord. This singing is not for its own sake but for God's sake, for the worship of God.

Conclusion

Sing to the Lord: Music in Divine Worship, the U.S. Bishops' document on liturgical music, underscores the significance of carefully prepared and authentically sung celebrations of the Sacred Liturgy. This book has provided a detailed and comprehensive study of the document so that priests, deacons, seminarians, and all liturgical music ministers can actually put into practice the principles and ideas set forth in *Sing to the Lord*. This study grounds these same practices and ideas in theological and liturgical foundations rooted in the liturgical books.

At the same time, we have also encouraged you to realize that there is always more understanding that can be provided, more explanations to be given, to promote the sung celebration of the Sacred Liturgy. Our aim with this book is to complement the aim of *Sing to the Lord*: to sing the Sacred Liturgy! In summary, we conclude with some general points as well as points specific to liturgical music ministers to ensure the continued application of *Sing to the Lord* in the Church in the United States.

GENERAL POINTS HELPFUL TO ALL

- *Sing to the Lord* does not replace the *Constitution on the Liturgy* or the *General Instruction of the Roman Missal*. It does replace its U.S. antecedents, *Music in Catholic Worship* and *Liturgical Music Today*. *Sing to the Lord*, the work of many and promulgated by the Bishops of the United States, continues and develops the catechesis on liturgical music found in universal ecclesial documents and the liturgical books for the Church in the United States. Diocesan workshops and parish information sessions on *Sing to the Lord* will further this necessary catechesis.

- *Sing to the Lord* proves the importance of continual liturgical updating, particularly in the understanding of what it means to sing the Sacred Liturgy rather than simply singing at the Liturgy.
- *Sing to the Lord* courageously addresses in our contemporary times the need to know why we sing, the formation and duties of all the members of the Church to sing the Liturgy, the value of the choir, the beauty of Gregorian chant, and the use of the texts and chants in the ritual books.

PARTICULAR POINTS HELPFUL TO LITURGICAL MUSIC MINISTERS

- Those involved in choosing music for the Sacred Liturgy need to consider the holiness of the music which presumes and proposes an authentic musical rendering of the texts.
- The ritual books for the Sacraments are the first resource to consider when choosing and planning music for these liturgical celebrations.
- Composers are encouraged to craft musical compositions drawn directly from the specific texts in the ritual books and to write music that accords with the nature of the specific part of the rite. For example, an acclamation is entirely different from a hymn or the manner in which a responsorial psalm is to be rendered.
- The need for liturgical-music catechesis cannot be emphasized enough. This catechesis includes particularly why we sing, who sings and what we sing. This ongoing catechesis, while the chief responsibility of the Bishop, for all the members of the Church, is indeed a personal duty of all who lead the People of God in liturgical song. Liturgical music ministers are encouraged to take *Sing to the Lord* and make it their own.

Overall, *Sing to the Lord* continues to guide the Church in the United States according to the plan for the renewal of singing liturgical music first announced by the Fathers of the Second Vatican Council. Although uneven at times in presentation and application, *Sing to the Lord's* strength lies in its charge to sing the Sacred Liturgy. Authentic liturgical music supports the Church's prayer by enriching its liturgical rites (see STL 15).

Sing to the Lord as a document addressed to all the members of the Church in the United States constitutes one of its additional strengths. This new document, as it updates previous statements on the liturgy and music, speaks to Bishops, priests, deacons, and all the faithful, especially liturgical music ministers, with a unilateral expectation that we engage in liturgical music for its formative and participative value to celebrate the Mysteries of the Lord.

We need *Sing to the Lord* today. The Bishops' new document and this companion are much needed guides to sing the Sacred Liturgy for the worship of Almighty God. Let us sing to the Lord!

Selected Bibliography

GENERAL SOURCES

Catechism of the Catholic Church. Second Edition. Libreria Editrice Vaticana, 2000.

The Liturgy Documents: A Parish Resource. Volume One. Chicago: Liturgy Training Publications, 1991.

The Liturgy Documents: A Parish Resource. Volume Two. Chicago: Liturgy Training Publications, 1999.

The Sixteen Documents of Vatican II. Introductions by Douglas G. Bushman. Edited by Marianne Lorraine Trouvé. Boston: Pauline Books and Media, 1999.

RITUAL BOOKS

Book of Blessings. New York: Catholic Book Publishing Company, 1989.

Holy Communion and Worship of the Eucharist Outside Mass. New York: Catholic Book Publishing Company, 1973.

Liturgy of the Hours. Volumes 1–4. New York: Catholic Book Publishing Company, 1975.

Missale Romanum ex decreto Sacrosancti Oecumenici Concilii Vaticani II instauratum auctoritate Pauli PP. VI promulgatum Ioannis Pauli PP. II cura recognitum, editio typica tertia. Città del Vaticano: Libreria Editrice Vaticana, 2002.

Pastoral Care of the Sick: Rites of Anointing and Viaticum. Bilingual Edition (Spanish). Chicago: Liturgy Training Publications, 2003.

Rite of Baptism for Children. New York: Catholic Book Publishing Company, 1973.

Rite of Christian Initiation of Adults. Chicago: Liturgy Training Publications, 2007.

Rite of Penance. New York: Catholic Book Publishing Company, 1975.

Rite of Marriage. New York: Catholic Book Publishing Company, 1973.

Rites of Ordination. Washington, DC: USCCB Publishing, 2003.

Order of Christian Funerals. New York: Catholic Book Publishing Company, 1999.

Order of Celebrating Marriage, Second Typical Edition, from the Roman Ritual, revised by decree of the Second Vatican Ecumenical Council published by authority of Pope Paul VI revised at the direction of Pope John Paul II. Unpublished English Translation, International Commission on English in the Liturgy, Washington DC, 1996.

The Roman Missal revised by decree of the Second Vatican Council and published by authority of Pope Paul VI: The Sacramentary. New York: Catholic Book Publishing Co., 1985.

The Roman Missal restored by decree of the Second Ecumenical Council of the Vatican and promulgated by authority of Pope Paul VI: Lectionary for Mass, Volume I: Sundays, Solemnities, Feasts of the Lord and the Saints. Second Typical Edition. Collegeville: The Liturgical Press, 1998.

The Roman Missal restored by decree of the Second Ecumenical Council of the Vatican and promulgated by authority of Pope Paul VI: Lectionary for Mass,

Volume IV: Common of Saints, Ritual Masses, Masses for Various Needs and Occasions, Votive Masses, and Masses for the Dead. Second Typical Edition. Collegeville: The Liturgical Press, 2002.

Sunday Celebrations in the Absence of a Priest: Leader's Edition. Prepared by the Committee on the Liturgy, National Conference of Catholic Bishops. New York: Catholic Book Publishing Co., 1994.

LITURGICAL MUSIC BOOKS

Graduale Romanum. Abbey of St. Peter of Solemnes, 1979.

*Graduale Simplex.*Rome: Libreria Editrice Vaticana, 1988.

Liber Hymnarius. Brewster, MA: Paraclete Press, 1983.

Mundelein Psalter, The. Douglas Martis, editor. Chicago/Mundelein, IL: Hillenbrand Books, 2007.

Ordo Cantus missae epitio typical acteria, Rome: Liberia Editrice Vaticana, 1988.

Sacrosanctum concilium, in The Liturgy.

ROMAN DOCUMENTS

Chirograph for the Centenary of the Motu Proprio "Tra le sollecitudini" on Sacred Music, 2003.

Christus Dominus in *The Sixteen Documents of Vatican II.* Introductions by Douglas G. Bushman. Edited by Marianne Lorraine Trouvé. Boston: Pauline Books and Media, 1999.

General Instruction on the Roman Missal. Washington, DC: USCCB Publishing, 2003. In, *Liturgy Documents, Vol. One, Fourth Edition.* Chicago: Liturgy Training Publications, 2004.

Liturgiam authenticam: On the Use of Vernacular Languages in the Publication of the Books of the Roman Liturgy, Boston: Daughters of St. Paul, 2003.

Musicam sacram. Rome: Libreria Editrice Vaticana, 1967.

Paschale solemnitas: On Preparing and Celebrating Easter Feasts, in *Liturgy Documents, Volume Two.* Chicago: Liturgy Training Publications, 2003.

Sacramentum caritatis. Rome: Libreria Editrice Vaticana, 2007.

Sacrosanctum concilium, in *The Liturgy Documents: A Parish Resource. Volume One.* Chicago: Liturgy Training Publications, 1991.

Tra le Sollecitudini, 1903. This can be found in *Papal Teachings: The Liturgy,* Boston: Daughters of St. Paul, 1962, pp. 177–187, and in Pamela Jackson, *An Abundance of Graces: Reflections of Sacrosanctum Concilium,* Chicago: Hillenbrand Books, 2004, pp. 116–123.

Varietates legitimae: Inculturation and the Roman Liturgy: Fourth Instruction for the Right Application of the Conciliar Constitution on the Liturgy (1994), In *The Liturgy Documents, Volume Two.* Chicago: Liturgy Training Publications, 1999.

Voluntari obsequens. Letter to the bishops on the minimum repertoire of plainchant, Sacred Congregation of Divine Worship, April 14, 1974 in *Notitiae,* April 1974, pp. 123–126.

U.S. Bishops' Documents

Built of Living Stones: Art, Architecture, and Worship, Washington, D.C.: United States Conference of Catholic.

Bishops, 2000. In, *Liturgy Documents, Vol.One, Fourth Edition*. Chicago: Liturgy Training Publications, 2004.

Co-Workers in the Vineyard of the Lord: A Resource for Guiding the Development of Lay Ecclesial Ministry, Washington, D.C.: United States Conference of Catholic Bishops, 2005.

Directory of Popular Piety and the Liturgy: Principles and Guidelines. Congregation of Divine Worship. Boston: Pauline Books and Media, 2003.

Guidelines for the Publication of Worship Aids, in Bishop's Committee on the Liturgy Newsletter, Vol. XXXIV, July/August 1998.

Liturgical Music Today. Washington, D.C.: Bishops' Committee on the Liturgy, National Conference of Catholic Bishops, 1982. In, *Liturgy Documents, Vol.One, Fourth Edition*. Chicago: Liturgy Training Publications, 2004.

Music in Catholic Worship, 2nd ed. Washington, D.C.: Bishops' Committee on the Liturgy, National Conference of Catholic.

Bishops, 1983. In, *Liturgy Documents, Volume One, Fourth Edition*. Chicago: Liturgy Training Publications, 2004.

Newsletter, Committee on the Liturgy of the United States Catholic Bishops. Volume XLII, November, 2006, p. 45–46;

Volume XLIII, August, 2007, p. 35; Volume XLIII, November-December, 2007, p. 47.

Policy for the Approval of Musical Compositions for the Liturgy, November, 1996. Bishop's Committee on the Liturgy Newsletter, Vol. XXXIII, January-February, 1997.

Sing to the Lord: Music in Divine Worship. United States Conference of Catholic Bishops. Washington, DC: USCCB Publishing, 2008.

Other Books

Joncas, Jan Michael, *From Sacred Song to Ritual Music.* Collegeville, MN: Liturgical Press, 1997.

Ruff, Anthony, OSB, Sacred Music and Liturgical Reform: Treasures and Transformations. Chicago, Mundelein, IL: Hillenbrand Books, 2007.

Schaefer, Edward, *Catholic Music through the Ages: Balancing the Needs of a Worshipping Church*. Chicago, Mundelein, IL: Hillenbrand Books, 2008.

Tietze, Christoph, *Hymn Introits for the Liturgical Year: The Origin and Development of the Latin Texts.* Chicago, Mundelein, IL: Hillenbrand Books, 2005.

Index

About the Author

REVEREND GERALD DENNIS GILL, a priest of the Archdiocese of Philadelphia, was ordained in 1983. Father Gill holds degrees in the Sacred Liturgy from Sant'Anselmo's Pontificio Istituto Liturgico in Rome. He served for 14 years as a parochial vicar in two large suburban parishes and one year as Associate Director of the Office of Worship in the Archdiocese of Philadelphia. He was professor of Sacred Liturgy at St. Charles Borromeo Seminary and Immaculata University. Most recently he completed a five-year term as the Director of Liturgy at the Pontifical North American College in Rome and is currently the Director of the Office of Divine Worship of Philadelphia.

Acknowledgments

Excerpts from the English translation of Rite of Baptism for Children © 1969, International Committee on English in the Liturgy, Inc. (ICEL); excerpts from the English translation of Rite of Marriage © 1969, ICEL; excerpts from the English translation of Rite of Penance © 1974, ICEL; the English translation of the Constitution on the Sacred Liturgy and *The General Instruction of the Liturgy of the Hours* from *Documents on the Liturgy. 1963–1979: Conciliar, Papal, and Curial Texts* © 1982, ICEL; excerpts from the English translation of *Pastoral Care of the Sick: Rites of Anointing and Viaticum* © 1982, ICEL; excerpts from the English translation of *Order of Christian Funerals* © 1985, ICEL; excerpts from the English translation of *Rites of Ordination of a Bishop, of Priests, and of Deacons* © 2000, 2002, ICEL; excerpts from the English translation of *The General Instruction of the Roman Missal* © 2002, ICEL. All rights reserved.

Msgr. Reynold Hillenbrand
1904-1979

Monsignor Reynold Hillenbrand, ordained a priest by Cardinal George Mundelein in 1929, was Rector of St. Mary of the Lake Seminary from 1936 to 1944.

He was a leading figure in the liturgical and social action movement in the United States during the 1930s and worked to promote active, intelligent, and informed participation in the Church's liturgy.

He believed that a reconstruction of society would occur as a result of the renewal of the Christian spirit, whose source and center is the liturgy.

Hillenbrand taught that, since the ultimate purpose of Catholic action is to Christianize society, the renewal of the liturgy must undoubtedly play the key role in achieving this goal.

Hillenbrand Books strives to reflect the spirit of Monsignor Reynold Hillenbrand's pioneering work by making available innovative and scholarly resources that advance the liturgical and sacramental life of the Church.